TRIBAL DEVELOPMENT PROGRAMMES AND SOCIAL TRANSFORMATION

TRIBAL DEVELOPMENT PROGRAMMES AND SOCIAL TRANSFORMATION

By

Dr. A. Naganna
M.A., M.Phil., Ph.D.
Deptt. of Sociology
Sri Krishnadevaraya University
Anantapur – 515 055
(Andhra Pradesh)

&

Prof. Ch. Umamohan
M.A., M.Phil., Ph.D.
Deptt. of Sociology
Sri Krishnadevaraya University
Anantapur – 515 055
(Andhra Pradesh)

DISCOVERY PUBLISHING HOUSE PVT. LTD.
NEW DELHI-110 002

Published by:
Tilak Wasan
DISCOVERY PUBLISHING HOUSE PVT. LTD.
4831/24, Ansari Road, Prahlad Street
Darya Ganj, New Delhi-110002 (India)
Phone: +91-11-23279245, 43764432
Fax: +91-11-23253475
E-mail: parul.wasan@gmail.com
discoverypublishinghouse@gmail.com
info@discoverypublishinggroup.com
web: www.discoverypublishinggroup.com

First Edition: 2011
ISBN: 978-81-8356-853-1

Tribal Development Programmes and Social Transformation

Printed at:
Shree Balaji Art Press
Delhi

PREFACE

This book 'Yerukulas: Social Exclusion and Social Inclusion is based on an extensive study of a denotified tribe.

Yerukulas are an ancient indigenous tribe in South India. They are predominantly spread in the status of Andhra Pradesh and Tamil Nadu. During the colonial period this tribe was made to suffer with undeliable social Stigma of Criminal Tribe, experienced Social Exclusion on account of the harsh policy of criminal tribes by the British rulers.

This book is a modest attempt to explore the valiant efforts of the community to erase there social stigma and the trends of there efforts for social inclusion. The study spans four generations and thus investigates the changing trends from the pre-independent British India to the present Independent India in the era of globalization. This works is a revised form of Ph.D. thesis by Dr. A. Naganna and accepted by Sri Krishnadevaraya University in 2008. It is our hope that the book is useful to scholars working in the areas of tribal and development studies, Sociology and Social Anthropology, Foklore. Our primary interest is to document the neglect of the indigenous tribes who live in the plains and their struggle for inclusion.

To take this opportunity to thank Prof. B. Subramanayam, Director, Centre for the Study of Social Exclusion and Social Inclusive Policy, Andhra University,

Visakhapatnam, Prof. Krishna Reddy, Department of Foklore Studies, Dravidian University, Kuppam, Dr. K. Nagaraju and our respondents for their encouragement. We all so thanks the publishers.

–Authors

Contents

Tribals constitute 8.2 per cent of India's population as per census of India 2001. They are reckoned as indigenous people. They are also reckoned as Dalits as they are neglected and are not part of the mainstream.

The issue of tribal development has become salient in the context of the democratic and liberal framework which has been adopted in India. The legitimacy of a democratic framework depends to a grate extent on its ability to meet the needs and aspirations of the most submerged, exploited and neglected sections of the society. Lack of concern for these sections would erode the very moral legitimacy that such a framework claims to possess. Needless to add, tribes constitute such a section of the society. They occupy the lowest rungs of social, economic and political structure of the society.

TRIBAL SCENARIO IN INDIA

The tribal population of the country, as per the 2001 census, is 8.43 crores, constituting 8.2 per cent of the total population. The population of tribes had grown at the rate of 24.45 per cent during the period 1991-2001. More than half the Scheduled Tribe population is concentrated in the States of Madhya Pradesh, Chhattisgarh, Maharashtra, Orissa, Jharkhand and Gujarat.

The main concentration of tribal population is in central India and in the North-eastern States. However, they have their presence in all states and Union Territories except Haryana, Punjab, Delhi, Puducherry, and Chandigarh.

Though, tribals are distributed all over the country one can identify a few concentration points such as Nagaland, Chota Nagapur, Nilagiri Hills etc. Roy Burman (1972) and Vidyarthi (1977) have suggested a more or less identical six-fold classification on the basis of regional distribution of the tribal population:

1. ***North-Eastern Region:*** In the States of Manipur, Arunachal Pradesh, Nagaland, Assam, Mizoram, Meghalaya etc. Tribes like the Abor, Garo, Khasi, Mizo, Naga, Mismi etc. who mostly belong to the Mongolian racial stock.
2. ***Himalayan Region:*** In the Sub-Himalayan regions covering parts of North Bengal, Uttar Pradesh and Himachal Pradesh tribes like Lepcha, Rabha etc. mostly belonging to Mongolian racial group.
3. ***Central India Region:*** In the older hills and Chota Nagpur Plateau, along the dividing Lines between Penisular India and the Indo-Gangetic basin live many tribal communities like the Bhumji, Gond, Ho, Oraon, Munda, Santhal etc. covering the states of Bihar, Orissa, Madhya Pradesh and West Bengal and mostly belonging to Proto-Australoid racial stock.
4. ***Western India Region:*** Covering the states of Rajasthan, Maharastra, Gujarat, Goa, Dadra and Nagar Haveli live a number of tribal communities, the most important of them being the Bhil racially belonging to the Proto-Australoid group.

6. ***Southern India Region:*** Covering the states of Karnataka, Andhra Pradesh, Tamil Nadu and Kerala, in the Nilgiri Hills and converging lines of the Ghats live the Chenchu, Kadar, toda etc. having Negrito, Caucasoid, Proto-Australoid or mixed Physical features.

6. ***Island Region:*** Covering Andaman, Nicobar and Lakshadweep Islands live a number of small tribes like Andamanese, Orge etc.

If one looks at the distribution of tribals a little more closely, an interesting feature emerges. In some states they constitute an overwhelming proportion of their population whereas in the whole country they form an insignificant percentage of population. For example, tribals constitute 83.99 per cent of populations in Nagaland but only 1.26 per cent of the total tribal population of India. Similarly in Mizoram they constitute 93.55 per cent of population but only 0.89 per cent of the total tribal population of India (*Chaudhri* 1982: xviii). This clearly indicates that in a number of States or Union Territories the tribals constitute the bulk of the population whereas in others, they are outnumbered by the non-tribals. This type of demographic variations is, however, bound to affect the socio-economic, political and cultural processes among the tribes.

The economic activities of tribals can be broadly categorised as food gathering (including hunting and fishing), pastoral, shifting hill cultivation, settled agriculture, handicrafts, trade and commerce, labour work including agriculture and industry.

Therefore, tribal development assumes importance and so are the studies on tribal communities and their development.

TRIBAL DEVELOPMENT AND THE FIVE YEAR PLANS

The Constitutional commitments prompted the Policy-makers and the Planners to accord high priority to the welfare and development of STs Right from the beginning of the country's developmental planning, launched in 1951.

The First Five-year Plan (1951-56) clearly laid down the principle that 'the general development programmes should be so designed to cater adequately to the Backward Classes and special provisions should be used for securing additional and more intensified development'.

The ***Second Five-year Plan (1956-61)*** envisaged that the benefits of economic development should accrue more and more to the relatively less privileged classes of society in order to reduce inequalities. As for the STs, 'Welfare

Programmes have to be based on respect and understanding of their culture and traditions and an appreciation of the social, psychological and economic problems with which they are faced'. This was in tune with *'Panchsheel'*—the Five Principles of Tribal Development - enunciated by the first Prime Minister, Pt. Jawaharlal Nehru. An important landmark during the Second Plan was the creation of 43 Special Multi-purpose Tribal Blocks (SMPTBs) later called Tribal Development Blocks (TDBs). Each was planned for about 25,000 people as against 65,000 in a normal block. An amount of Rs.15 lakh per SMPTB was contributed by the Central Government. The Committee on SMPTBs set up under the Chairmanship of Verrier Elwin (1959) studied the working of these blocks and found that they were providing very useful services.

The Third Five-year Plan (1961-66) advocated the principle to establish greater 'equality of opportunity' and to bring about reduction in disparities in income and wealth and a more even distribution of economic power. While appraising the programmes of the Third Plan the Shilu Ao Study Team remarked that 'if progress is to be judged by what remains to be done to bring the tribals on par with the rest of the populations, the leeway is still considerable.

The Fourth Five-year Plan (1969-74) proclaimed that the 'basic goal was to realise rapid increase in the standard of living of the people through measures which also promote equality and social justice'. An important step was setting up of six pilot projects in Andhra Pradesh, Bihar, Madhya Pradesh and Orissa in 1971-72 as Central Sector Scheme with the primary objective of combating political unrest and Left Wing extremism. A separate Tribal Development Agency was established for each project. The Fourth Plan outlay for each was Rs.1.50 crore for the core programmes of economic development and Rs. 0.50 crore for arterial roads. These agencies were later merged with Integrated Tribal Development Projects during the Fifth Plan.

The Fifth Five-year Plan (1974-78) marked a shift in the approach as reflected in the launching of Tribal Sub-Plan (TSP) for the direct benefit of the development of Tribals. The TSP stipulated that funds of the State and Centre should be quantified on the population proportion basis, with budgetary mechanisms to ensure accountability, non-divertability and utilisation for the welfare and development of STs. With this thrust the concept of Tribal Sub-Plan came into action during the Fifth Plan. There has been a substantial increase in the flow of funds for the development of STs under this arrangement, resulting in the expansion of infrastructure facilities and enlargement of coverage of the target groups in the beneficiary oriented programmes.

The Sixth Five-year Plan (1980-85) was sought to ensure a higher degree of devolution of funds so that at least 50 per cent of tribal families were provided assistance to cross the poverty line. Emphasis was on family-oriented economic activities rather than infrastructure development schemes. A "Modified Area Development Approach" (MADA) was devised for pockets of tribal concentration with population of 10,000; at least half of them being STs, and 245 MADA pockets were delineated. Also, 20 more tribal communities were identified as 'primitive', raising the total to 72.

In the Seventh Five-year Plan (1985-90), there was substantial increase in the flow of funds for the development of STs, resulting in the expansion of infrastructural facilities and enlargement of coverage. Emphasis was laid on the educational development of STs. For the economic development of SCs and STs, two national level institutions were set up *viz.*, (*i*) Tribal Cooperative Marketing Development Federation (TRIFED) in 1987 as an apex body for State Tribal Development Cooperative Corporations; and (ii) National Scheduled Castes and Scheduled Tribes Finance and Development Corporation (NSFDC) in 1989. The former was envisaged to provide remunerative price for the Forest and Agriculture Produce of tribals while the latter was intended to provide credit support for employment generation.

In the Eighth Five-year Plan (1992-97), efforts were intensified to bridge the gap between the levels of development of the STs and those of other sections of the society so that by the turn of the century, these disadvantaged sections of the Population could be brought on par with the rest of the society. The Plan not only emphasised elimination of exploitation but also paid attention to the special problems of suppression of rights, land alienation, non-payment of minimum wages and restrictions on right to collect minor forest produce etc. Attention, on priority basis, continued to be paid for the socio-economic upliftment of STs. A review of tribal development in early nineties revealed that 'Though the TSP Strategy has yielded results, yet were not in a position to commensurate with the efforts put in and investments made'. However, the allocation for development of STs was increased during this plan period also.

In the Ninth Five-year Plan (1997-2001), envisaged advancement of STs through a process of empowerment, wherein efforts are to be made to create an enabling environment conductive for the exercise of their rights freely, enjoyment of the privileges and leading a life of self confidence and dignity at par with the other citizens of the country. This encompasses vital components namely

1. Social empowerment,
2. Economic empowerment,
3. Social Justice.

In the Tenth Five-year Plan (2002-07), An outlay of Rs.1200 crores is provided for the Tenth Plan for the Welfare of Scheduled Castes and Scheduled Tribes, out of which an amount of Rs.1044.16 crores is provided for SCs and Rs.155.84 crores for STs for both ongoing and new schemes. The major programmes-wise details are indicated in Table 1.1. (See Table on page 12)

Education

The objective for educational advancement of SCs and STs include improving the literacy rate, female literacy rate, universal education, improving the educational status, increasing the enrolment rate, reducing dropout rate repetition and retention rate at all levels, improving the pass percentage in X and XII Stds., improving the performance on competitive examinations, improving the quality of teaching and encouraging the integration of ST with the rest of the society. The thrust will be on the large involvement of the community through active participation of the parent-teacher associations, local bodies, activists/volunteers and NGOs, strengthening of formation and functioning of PTAs, imparting training to school students after completion of schooling and absorbing them as teachers for primary sections, constitution of school-management committees to supervise the improvement of school infrastructure, creating better teaching-learning atmosphere and monitoring the quality of education. For achieving universal education, the facilities provided under DPEP and Sarva Sikhsha Abhiyan Programmes will be utilised for strengthening schools/ hostel infrastructure. They include construction of additional class rooms, labs, and provisions of lab equipment's better teaching learning materials, playgrounds, sports material, and provision of water facilities, sanitary facilities and upgrading of schools wherever possible. For the promotion of tribal education, special emphasis will be laid on opening of more number of GTR schools, enhancing grants to ashram school, establishing vocational training institutes, stepping up of community participation in education, establishing close relationship with the tribes, opening of non-formal education and evening schools in tribal areas. The following are the new schemes under Education:

- Captive Teacher Training Programmes for SCs/STs
- Strengthening the Monitoring Mechanisms through Local Participation
- Acquisition of Land for Schools
- Provision of Lab and Lab Equipments
- Extension of Computer Education to High Schools
- Promotion of Private Management Schools to Benefit SC/ST

- Promotion of Private Sector Participation in Hostel Management
- Assistance to Students Staying in Hostels run by Private Institutions/ College/Universities.

Economic Development

The objectives will be to reduce the percentage of SC/ST families living below poverty line to less than 10 per cent and to raise the economic status of this segment of the population. The strategies will be towards mobilising and organising the poor SC and ST families in Self-help Groups (SHGs), crating awareness on literacy and health care, improving the capacity and ability of poor people to manage risks, promoting self reliance and thrift, supporting in infrastructure, forward and backward linkages and other assistance for improvement in the income generating capacity of SC and ST families living below poverty line, improving thee skills of SCs/STs by providing training and identification of appropriate institutions and activities, imparting wide range captive job-oriented vocational training to the educated unemployed through EDP, promoting income generating capacities in industry/ secondary sector and service sector thereby providing mobility from low income areas of primary sector to high income areas of secondary and services sector, imparting entrepreneurial skills and giving financial and non-financial support to the SCs/STs to start small and medium scale enterprises in industrial and service sectors. The following are the new schemes under Economic Development:

- Special Economic Development Programme
- Skill Development/ Building Training to Below Poverty Line Families for the Promotion of Micro Enterprises
- Venture Capital Funding
- Vocational Training
- Talent Search Training Programme for Job Placements in Private Sector.

Housing and Other Activities

The main objectives will be to fulfil the housing needs of these communities and to reduce the gap in the provision of basic amenities between Schedule Castes habitations, to improve the health and nutritional status of Scheduled Castes/ Scheduled Tribes population, to recognise the tribal forest rights, especially the ownership of minor forest production, to prevent/ prohibit land alienation of tribal lands for which rules and regulations will be strictly followed while transferring the tribal lands to non-Tribals. The strategies will include assignment of house site pattas, construction of houses, provision of basic amenities like drinking water, link roads, electricity, street lights to the SC/ST habitations and provision of burial ground and pathways to burial ground to all the adi-dravidar habitations. The other activates include strengthening of ICDS scheme to the lactating women to meet the health and nutritional needs, creating awareness on modern healthcare and sanitation facilities to tribal population. The following are the new schemes under Housing and other Activities:

- Special Self-sufficiency Programme
- Hut Light Programme
- Housing for Adi-dravidars Engaged in Unclean Occupation.

Special Component Plan

The Special Component Plan for Scheduled Castes constitutes a distinct feature of the planning process in the country and is intended to comprehensively cover economies, educational and social development along with the fulfilment of minimum needs and human resources development. There is, in the main, two aspects in the flow of resources to the Special Component Plan, firstly the direct flow through development and secondly, the flow to the programme for scheduled castes through provision of social services, infrastructure and other facilities.

The Special Component Plan mechanism was evolved during the Sixth Plan to channels the flow of benefits from the State Plan for the development of Scheduled Castes in physical and financial terms. These programmes have been designed to help poor Scheduled Caste families through composite income generating programmes and to cover all the major occupational groups among Scheduled Castes such as agricultural labourers, labourers below poverty line etc., Further, the Special Component Plan seeks to improve the living conditions of Scheduled Castes through provision of drinking water supply, link-roads, house-sites and housing, primary schools, health centers veterinary centers, community halls, nutrition centers, extension of electricity etc., in the Scheduled Caste habitations.

TRIBAL SUB PLAN

The Tribal Sub Plan was introduced to ensure that all general development sectors at the State level earmark funds in proportion to ST population so that adequate benefits from all the concerned sectors flow to the tribal groups. The objective of the Tribal Sub Plan is to assist the Tribal families in improving their socio-economic and educational status. Economic Development Programmes in the fields of horticulture, animal husbandry, soil-conservation, minor irrigation, sericulture, small industries, bee-keeping etc. and area oriented development programmes like provision of drinking water, formation of roads, electrification, providing education and health facilities, improving forestry, communication, co-operation, social services etc. are taken up. The expenditure incurred for implementing the Tribal Sub Plan including the Special Central Assistance has increased steadily from Rs.94 lakhs in 1976-77 to Rs.17.55 crores in 2000-2001.

Tribal Sub Plan (TSP) strategy, which came into being in the Fifth Five Year Plan with the twin objectives of area and sectoral approaches, envisages protection of the interests of the Scheduled Tribal through legal and administrative measures and development and welfare activities through plan efforts. Empowerment of these historically disadvantaged tribal people requires more provision of the basic capabilities for integrating them into growth process.

The Tribal Sub Plan has been under implementations since 1976-77 with the aim of (1) helping the Scheduled Tribe families to cross the poverty line and (2) to provide basic amenities and facilities in their areas. The size of the Tribal Sub Plan should be in proportion to Scheduled Tribe population to the States total population. As far as Tamil Nadu is concerned, the flow to Tribal Sub Plan should be not less than 1.03% of the State Plan outlay.

The tenth plan approach paper has adopted an approach to ensure that the tribal economy is protected and supported against threats from the external markets. The ownership patent rights of the tribal people in respect of minor forests products vis-à-vis the use medical plants will be protected as per the provision of the intellectual property rights.

The primitive tribal groups are leading an extremely precarious existence and some of them are on the verge of extinction. An action plan incorporating total food and nutrition, health, security education facilities etc. will be prepared by the Centre/state governments. The proposed action plan will have an in built flexibility to cater to the specific needs of each such tribal and its environment.

For the primitive tribal groups, plain areas tribal groups, detailed plans will be prepared for their economic development, as for as possible, with the family as the unit, infrastructure and other developmental needs will be specifically identified. The integrated plan of development programme will be developed which take into account the social and economic organisation of life of these communities, their interests, aptitudes and abilities.

The percentage of outlays for tribal development during the planning period are presented in Table 1.1. As compared with the First Five Year plan, the total investment made for

Table 1.1. Percentage of plan outlay and expenditure for Tribal Development Programmes

SI No.	Plan	Years	Total Budget (Rs. in Crores)	Out lay Tribal Develo-pment progra-mmes (Rs. in (Crores)	Perc-entage
1.	I Plan	1951-56	1960.00	19.93	1.02
2.	II Plan	1956-61	4600.00	49.92	1.08
3.	III Plan	1961-66	8576.00	50.53	0.60
4.	Annual Plan	1966-69	6756.00	32.32	0.48
5.	IV Plan	1969-74	15902.00	75.00	0.47
6.	V Plan	1974-79	37250.00	1182.00	0.32
7.	Annual Plan	1979-80	12176.00	855.16	7.02
8.	VI Plan	1980-85	97500.00	4193.00	4.30
9.	VII Plan	1985-90	180000.00	6976.76	3.86
10.	VIII Plan	1991-95	314576.43	18311.93	5.82
11.	IX Plan	1997-2002	859200.00	775.00	0.09

Source: Planning Commission Report on Welfare of SC/ST and Other BCs, Government of India, New Delhi. 2000-02\

tribal development programmes has been increased form 44 times to the Fifth Five-year Plan to 200 times to the Sixth Plan further increased to 280 times to the Seventh Plan and 332 times to the Eighth Five Year Plan increased as a result of operation of new strategy on Tribal Sub-plan improve the quality of living conditions of the tribals in the tribal area.

The tribal sub plan area is divided into 194 operational units termed as Integrated Tribal Development Project (ITDA) in blocks where scheduled Tribe population is more than 50 per cent of the total population and 259 Modified Area Development Approach (MADA). In addition 82 clusters with a total population of 5000 of which 50 per cent are Scheduled Tribes in each cluster and 75 Primitive Tribal Groups (PTGs) have been identified. The special central assistance is an additive to the state plan and programme for Scheduled Caste and Scheduled Tribe for income generating schemes, training and institutional build-up. Besides there are a number of centrally sponsored schemes which have been undertaken for the benefit of Scheduled Tribes. Apart from these, some schemes under the non-plan sector have also been undertaken by the Central and the state governments for the advancement of the tribal communities.

Thus, a number of development programmes for the tribals have been launched in the five-year plans.

But it was only in the fifth plan that a landmark event happened. For the first time, the concept of sub-plan for the tribal region of a state within the overall framework of the State plan was initiated.

The tribal sub-plan approach initiated in the fifth plan continued in the Sixth Plan. The main objective was to narrow the gap between the level of development of tribal areas and others and to improve the quality of life of the tribal people. To achieve this, different economic programmes and protective measures having a bearing on their employment, education and health services were initiated.

Despite the fact that the needs of the tribals being very different from the rest of their brethren, yet the development of Scheduled Tribes was made part of the Backward Classes Sector which handled the welfare and development of SCs, STs, OBCs and Minorities till very recently. It was only in October 1999, an exclusive Ministry of Tribal Affairs was set up under the charge of a fullfledged Cabinet rank Minister to attend to the following mandate:

(*i*) Tribal Welfare—Planning, Policy formulation, Research and Training.

(*ii*) Tribal development including scholarships to STs

(*iii*) Promotion of voluntary efforts in development of STs

(*iv*) Administrative Ministry with respect to matters concerning:

- Scheduled areas;
- Autonomous districts of Assam excluding roads and bridge works and ferries thereon;
- Regulations framed by Governors of State for Scheduled areas for Tribal areas specified in Part A of Table appended to paragraph 20 of the Sixth Schedule to the Constitution;
- National Commission for Scheduled Castes and Scheduled Tribes in so far as they relate to STs; and
- Issue of directions with regard to drawing up and execution of schemes essential for the welfare of Scheduled Tribes.

Thus, the newly set up Ministry of Tribal Affairs has become the Nodal Ministry and was made responsible for empowering STs and thus raises their over-all status on par with the rest of the society. The Ministry in its nodal capacity is expected to i) formulate policies and programmes; ii) enacts/amends legislations affecting STs and iii) co-ordinates the efforts of both governmental and non-governmental organisations working to improve the lot of STs in the country.

Despite the various development programmes, the conditions of tribals continue to remain quite unsatisfactory. Poverty still remains a major issue calling for a serious attention from the development agencies. Health, education, infrastructural and communication facilities are still in a rudimentary state. One more issue which has become extremely important in the contemporary tribal world to be examined is the issue of identity. One notices a heightened sense of ethnic / cultural consciousness among tribals. Exploitation from outsiders continues unabated. The so-called development programmes instead of improving the conditions have actually worsened them. For example, the establishment of big dams and projects ostensibly for the purpose of facilitating development has actually dispossessed tribals of their control over the forests (which constituted the secondary source of livelihood) and led to further economic impoverishment. On the basis of empirical examination, one tends to conclude that development programmes have not benefited the tribal communities; sometimes development had been at the cost of tribal interests. Because of the skewed development process, one notices aggravation of socio-economic inequalities among tribals themselves. The emergence of elites among tribals is illustrative of this.

Despite so much emphasis being given on the development of tribal nothing much significant seems to have happened to the actual living conditions of tribals. In fact, the socio-economic conditions have worsened due to the skewed development process. This is reflected in a number of scholarly studies conducted on the tribal development in India (Mahapatra 1972; Vidyarthi 1981; Burman 1986; Ashish Bose *et al.* 1990; Imchen 1990; Pathy 1998; Thakur 2001; Singh 2002; Sinha 2002 to mention a few).

This is because the basic issues concerning tribal development have not been properly appreciated.

REVIEW OF LITERATURE

Various studies on the transitional aspects of different tribals have figures in the history of Indian Anthropology. Most of the monographs on Indian tribes written from the beginning of the twentyfirst century by the British Ethnographies, Administrators and some Indian Sociologists and Anthropologists.

E.T. Dalton (1872) compiled and completed the data on the geographical settings physical traits, economic, social and religions life of the Lepchas and Linps of Sikkim and Darjeeling. W. Crookes (1897) in his study described the culture of the tribes like the Bhutias the Gujjars, the Jharus and the Khagas. The study brought out the tribals reciprocal interaction with economy and social life. D.N. Muzundar (1937) carried field work and presented a comprehensive study and brought out the characteristics.

Elwin's (1951) study on the savars dealt with the religious aspects of the primitive tribes that led them to develop the concept of Spiritualism. The myths and legends which were rightly observed by him as tribal puranas, brought a turning point in the history of tribal studies. The census operations of the Government of India also intensified the schemes of tribal studies during the 1961 census which are still continues and have brought out monographs on tribal culture in different parts of India.

S.C. Roy (1972) in one of his studies on tribals, took a humanitarian interest especially in the Mundas of Chotanagapur. He studied their language and also published a monograph on mundas and their country.

Vidyarthi (1976) discussed the observations on the Jarawa, the great Andamanese (a dying community), the Onge (also a dying group) the Shom Pen, the Chowra Hotchu, the Tarerssa Hotchu, and the Car Nicobarese. The author thinks that right beginning has been made to develop these people. The tempo of change, however, slow, makes suggestions about the development of natural and human resources. He shows particular concern of the communities which are faced with extinction.

Asha G. Mane (1981) in his study explained that the Gonds are found to be distributed in Madhya Prades, Orissa, Maharashtra, Andhra Pradesh, Bihar, Gujarat, Karnataka and West Bengal. The highest concentration in 1961 and 1971 is found in Madhya Pradesh 78 per cent, Orissa 10 per cent Maharashtra 7 per cent, Andhra Pradesh, Bihar, Gujarat, Karnataka and West Bengal combinedly show 40.5 per cent. They are in four endogamous tribes *viz.* Raj Gond, Madia, Dhurve and Khatulwar gonds. They enjoyed the status of rulers even before the present century. Gondi is widely spoken and remained the mother tongue of primary importance among them in the hilly and forest tract. It is mainly spoken in the proper Central Provinces and neighbouring tract of the Central. They think that the education is merely an entertainment for them. Monogamous marriage is common among the Gonds but polygamy is not altogether unknown. Family is patrilineal and partrilocal.

Chanda and Loknath Soni (1982) strongly felt that tribals are inarticulate and helpless. Through the reports of various tribal research institute organisations, we rarely get a true picture of the recent state of socio-economic condition of tribal of Vidarbha region and moreover whatever type of information we use to get they are also not analytical having aside few tribal groups who are somewhat called well-off in their economic position, bulk of tribal population in Maharashtra as a whole are still living at below subsistence level. Moreover, they are not in position to find out an alternative way to come out from their poor socio-economic condition. The development and welfare activity of the Government is very slow and disproportionate and the basic facilities which have been provided to them by the Government are very insufficient in comparison to the numerical strength of tribal population in a articular area. Surely, in course of our 30 years of Independence, this is no doubt a very poor achievement. Welfare work among the tribals in Vidarbha region has not progressed to the extent desired. It is perhaps due to lack of workers willing and ready to go and to live among the tribes and to do welfare activities among them. Maharastra Government, Central Government as well as other types of research organisations should come forward immediately with some welfare schemes and to do some welfare activities for those poor tribal communities, who are lingering behind.

Sibir R. Das (1979) in his study explained that the tribals, in an ideal sense, are often described as nearly self-sufficient in economy, social relation, and in contents of their culture, but in actual situation it is seen that they have relations with neighbouring castes and comminutes. The relationship at different levels of social actions where tribals and other castes participate is described. The field investigation was earned out in Koraput district of Orissa where the main ethnic groups are the Gadabas (a tribal group), Harijan, Ganda Rana, Mali, Dora and other castes. The prolonged contact of Gadabas with caste groups has made them conscious of their position and as a result they are adapting various ritual and cultural modes of the non-tribals to elevate their position and improve their social ties with Hindus.

S.C. Roy (1972) in one his studies on tribals took a humanitarian interest especially in the Mundas of Chotanagapur. He studied their language and also published a monograph on Mundas and their country.

Tribal Problems: Furer Haimendorf, C.V. (1941), one of the eminent Anthropologists, first studied the tribal problems of Hyderabad. Haimendorf explained the primitive economy of the chenchus and related in to their seasonal nomodism, Furer Haimendorf, C.V. (1945) then described the fortunes of the primitive tribes. His monograph in two volumes is on the Reddys of the Bison Hills, written in collaboration with his wife Elizabeth. Furer Haimendorf, C.V. (1948) presented the first full-length account of the present culture of Rajgonda. Later he wrote on the Pradhans, the guards of the Gowdas (1950-51).

With the inspiration and encouragement of Haimendorf, several scholars did research on these tribes. Mention among them may be made of Gulam Ahamad Khan (1942) who wrote a long paper on the chenchus, P.C. Reddy's (1940) study on the tribes, Haimendorf (1947) attempted a study of the tribal problems of Hyderabad. He studied the primitive economy of the chenchus and related it to their seasonal nomadism. He also studied the Reddis of Bison Hills (1945) and presented a full-length account of the culture of Raj Gonds (1948) and made another study on the Pradhans, who are the guards of Raj Gondas (1950-51).

Yanadi. Sayed Khwaja Mahboob Hussain (1950-51) who gave a descriptive account of the medicines among the Gowdas, the Kolans and the Chenchus. R.P. Rao (1952-53) studied the nomadic trading and stock-breeding Lambadis.

Tribal Unrest: The studies of Meggill (1964) G.P. Murdock (1968) Unrest is common among tribals owing to various problems including secure exploitation. A study of U.N. Mauin Kurue (1968) touched upon the tribal unrest in Andhra Agency. The study probed in detailed and found how the unrest developed in the minds of tribals and its consequences. V.M. Nair (1968) also explained Girijana revolt against Marxist way by Andhra tribals. In 1970-71, a tribal revolt motivated by communist and Marxist elements in Srikakulam district created a serious situation. M.Y. Naidu (1972) and N. Subha Reddy (1977) described the role of Naxalite movement in the tribal areas of Srikakulam district.

Strategies and Programmes for Tribal Development

As regarding the strategies and programmes for tribal development in India, the studies at macro level include those of B. Singh (1980), Roy-Burman (1980), Srivastava (1980). K.P. Singh (1988) Behru (1993) Saibaba and Rajendra Naidu (1992) focussed their attention on tribal development strategies in A.P. In these studies it was observed that the results achieved under TSP strategy were not commensurate with the expectations as well as investments made so far. Further, it was found in the study that there had been too much emphasis on quantitative investments rather than qualitative achievements.

B.K. Roy Burnan (1987) investigated the role of the State in the development of tribals. The study listed out different state policies and programmes for the uplift of the tribal people. S.S. Negi's book (1988) on "Tribal Welfare Development Administration" dealt with all aspects of development of tribals including their problems and constitutional provisions. B.D. Sarm's (1989) study revealed the planning of various issues in connection with development of Indian Tribals. R.R. Prasad's (1988) study found that the tribal development of India and strategies and programmes. B. Singh (1983-84) in his study examined the functions of the plans and programmes of the state for the development of tribals.

Gopal Rao (1981) attempted to study the impact made by the extension staff of the Girijan Development Agency (GDA) on the tribal farmers of Srikakulam District of Andhra Pradesh. While implementing the agriculture and animal husbandry programmes launched by the agencies. The author observed that in spite of the heavy expenditure on the schemes and development of more contingency administrative and extension staff. But failed to realised the benefits by the tribals to the desired extent. According to him the factors inhabiting the diffusion of farm innovations among the tribals are target-oriented planning of development programmes rather than clientele-oriented, ineffective use of extension methods, lack of missionary zeal among the extension workers, inadequate knowledge of extension staff of the cultural background of the people for whose benefit they are working. He further suggested that in order to make the developmental programmes, meaningful and successful among the tribals, there should be close contact between the extension workers and their clients. Otherwise, the entire development programmes involving millions of rupees in the tribal areas will become an exercise in futility.

Developmental Programmes and Their Impact: As regards implementation of developmental programmes and their impact on the living conditions of tribal people, there are several studies, for example, Khaun (1982) examined the implementation of programmes in North-Eastern region, Sharma (1983) conducted a study on implementation of programmes for dispersed tribals in the country. Mishra *et. al.* (1993) studied the implementation of programmes in Orissa, Krishna Reddy and Ramachandra Reddy (1991) evaluated the impact of programmes on Sugali tribe in Kurnool district Andhra Pradesh.

B. Chandhari's (1983) study dealt with Tribal Development in India. It covered different aspects of the tribal development. S.G. Deogankar (1980) studied the problems of development of tribal areas. The study revealed the difficulties being faced by the policymakers and administrators.

Tribe's Economy of Andhra Pradesh: Various studies have been made on the tribe's economy of Andhra Pradesh. A. Radhakrishna Murthy (1968) studies the tribal economy in the Andhra Agency. In his study, he explained the conditions of tribal economy, stages of development as well as their exploitation. D.V. Ragava Rao (1971) studied the indebtedness in a tribal society. According to him indebtedness is a major problem of the tribal people. He also explained different ways by which the tribals were exploited by the moneylenders.

T. Laxmaiah (1984) analysed socio-economic development of tribals. The study examined the economic level of tribals. D. Thakur (1986) also studied the socio-economic conditions of Indian tribes.

Tribal Development in Andhra Pradesh: As far as the tribal development in Andhra Pradesh is concerned, the studies are less in number, Palnaik (1971) studied Andhra Pradesh and Orissa states in relation to social conflicts and development in tribal areas.

P.S.K. Menon (1979) Padmanabha (1983) G.P. Reddy (1972) D.R. Prathap(1976) are some of the important to mention focussing on tribals' customs, rituals and the status in their economy.

P. Satyanarayana's (1973) study reviewed the tribal welfare programmes and their impact on the tribals. Satyanarayana (1976) tried to study the social welfare of the agency people of Andhra Pradesh. The study further spelt out the effects of the Government programmes for tribal development.

K.M. Rao's (1983) study attempts to examine the socio-cultural factors in the development of tribal areas.

P. Ramaiah's (1988) study described the role of Integrated Tribal Development Agency and Girijana Co-operative in the developments of tribals. The study also pointed out the importance of agriculture and forestry in the economy of tribals of Andhra Pradesh.

Bapuju (1974) analysed the working of the special standing committees on tribal welfare in Zilla Parshad of Visakhapatnam, Andhra Pradesh. According to the Statute the Standing Committee is only an advisory body to the Zilla Parishad and it has no powers to initiate or administer policies. The Zilla Parishad delegated only the power to review and sanction the tribal welfare schemes of Zilla Parishad and Government implemented tribal areas committees role in changing the conditions of the tribal people is limited by the statute itself. The task of tribal uplift is a complex one, which involves in the participation of various departments. The composition of the Committee predominantly with tribal members is an act of breaking the past and introducing a new turn in the history of tribal welfare of the district since the government and Zilla Parishad launching several programmes for the emancipation of this downtrodden masses, the tribal members of the Standing Committee should try to follow the stock of the present trend to break through the vicious circle of backwardness that struck the roots of the tribal community since the long past.

It is clear from the above studies that majority them have focussed their attention on tribal culture, beliefs, customs and religious practices. While few other studies have dealt, with the tribal welfare and development in India as the main theme.

Social Change: Mishara (1993) observed that social change is taking place in different directions and different degrees in tribal societies in India. Further, according to him there seems to be some resistance to change by the tribals because of certain factors. It was rightly pointed out that the protectionistic policies, uneven development and tribal exploitation, forest policy, displacement and alienation, educational policy, political socialisation etc. have promoted primordial loyalties among the tribals to make them apprehensive of the rest of India.

S.L. Kalia, (1961) made a conceptual study and attempted to test the concept of Sanskritisation and proposed the idea of tribalisation. It found in the study that the non-tribals living in the predominantly tribal areas are troubling themselves by accepting non-vegetarian food, alcoholic drinks and above all accepting the several religion functions of the tribals.

S.K. Srivastva (1958), conducted a field work on the Tarus of Nainital, tribals who claim themselves to be of Kshatriya origin. He developed the concept of Kashtriyalation to account for the changes in the tribal society.

Munirathnam Reddy (1979) discussed the problem of structural and functional identities of the ethnic groups inhabiting the hill tracts of Visakhapatnam district in coastal Andhra. He opined that social mobility and changing affiliations of these sub-tribes in the context of inter-ethnic relationships are of anthropological interest from both theoretical and practical points of view.

STATEMENT OF PROBLEM

It is clear from the above studies that majority them have focussed their attention on tribal culture, beliefs, customs and religious practices and cultural change. While few other studies have dealt, with the tribal welfare and development in India as the main theme.

These communities were secluded and were kept under strict watch and vigil. After the independence this act was repealed in the year 1952. Yet these communities continue to experience the social stigma of criminality. In addition to their dalit status, owning to *the social stigma* of criminality these communities are shunned by the society and experience social exclusion. During the last fifty five years several developmental programmes were launched for the benefit of the marginalised and the dalits. These developmental programmes have initiated the process of social inclusion and the social transformation.

In Andhra Pradesh, Yerukula community is one such stigmatised tribe. Yerukula's economic organisation is very simple and undifferentiated. Their primary occupation is basket making besides, they are engaged in several other occupations includes food gathering reasons of domestic animals and so on. Yerukula women are good fortunetellers, Venkateswarlu (1995; 237). They make money by using this skill. There were a lot of changes among these people over a period of time most of them started new economic pursuits. They have taken agriculture and other occupations for earning their livelihood some of then acquired education and entered into the public services.

A few studies were made on Yerukula tribe's social transformation (SimhadryYC (1973, 1974, 1974, 1979) Shashi (1995), Lalitha (1995) but these studies did not examine the social transformation in terms of social exclusion and social inclusion frame work. The deprivation of these groups is closely linked with the processes of caste and ethnicity-based exclusion and discrimination Amartya Sen draws attention to various meanings and dimensions of the concept of social exclusion (Sen 2000).

In view of the above reflections an attempt is made to study the social transformation of Yerukula community, a primitive tribal community which carries social stigma. The social transformation of this community is examined in the *conceptual frame work of social exclusion and inclusion* with reference to change and continuity in the areas of livelihood opportunities (occupational changes); educational levels; healthcare access; social participation; and perception of their status. The study is carried out in the context Rayalaseema region of Andhra Pradesh. Yerukulas are a primitive and numerically large community spread in Andhra Pradesh and neighbouring states like Tamil Nadu, Karnataka, and Maharastra.

CONCEPTS AND CLARIFICATIONS

Concept of Stigma

Erving Goffman described Stigma as a quality that significantly discredits an individual in the eyes of others

(*Goffman* 1963). Stigma is generally considered to be an attribute used to separate affected individuals from the normalized social order (*Gilmore* and *Somerville* 1994).The separation implies a process of devaluation and discrimination against stigmatized group (*Gilmore* and *Somerville* 1994).

Link and Phelam (2001) proposed a conceptual framework of stigma. In their model, stigma is a process during which five interrelated components converge. The five components include labelling; stereotyping; separation; status loss; and discrimination (systematic disapproval, rejection, and exclusion towards labelled individuals). According to the model, stigmatisation is wholly contingent on access to social, economic and political power that allows the identification of differences, the construction of stereotypes, the separation of labeled persons into distinct categories and the full execution of disapproval, rejection, exclusion and discrimination.

The sociology and social psychology literature on stigma is replete with characterisations of the stigmatic process. The definition offered by a recent survey of this literature is particularly useful here because it addresses the social as well as the psychological aspects of stigma. Stigma is characterised in terms of four interrelated components.

In the first component, people distinguish and label human differences.In the second, dominant cultural beliefs link labeled persons to undesirable characteristics to negative stereotypes. In the third, labeled persons are placed in distinct categories so as to accomplish some degree of separation of "us" from "them". In the forth, labelled persons experience status loss and discrimination that leads to unequal outcomes. Link and Phelan (2001, p. 367)

Stigma has both micro and macro social consequences. Link and Phelan assert that research on stigma has attended primarily to its perception by individuals and its consequences for micro-level interactions. On the other hand, stigmatic markers classify entire groups of individuals. The aggregate of behaviours which respond to stigmatic markers has systemic implications for aggregate social and economic performance.

Both individual characteristics and individual behaviours are available for stigmatic representation. The stigmatisation of race, gender, physical disabilities, mental illness and other characteristics is morally repugnant, and a continuing source of social ills. But the stigmatisation of behaviours is the central mechanism for enforcing social norms. Stigma is thus essential to the production of what some call 'social capital'. Stigma enforces social norms by stigmatising non-normative behaviour. Here this mechanism is modelled in order to draw some conclusions about its efficacy. A concrete instance of the social control process modelled here is the stigmatisation of certain kinds of criminals. Small-town newspapers routinely publish the names of those arrested (and not yet convicted) for driving under the influence of alcohol. Fears of public exposure are a strong incentive for tax compliance in some communities. But if everyone cheated or everyone drank, the social costs of exposure would be small.

The stigma mechanism suggests a coordination game, with high and low-activity equilibria. In the high-activity equilibrium, many people cheat, and so the stigma costs of cheating are small cheating is not stigmatised. The low-activity equilibria have few cheaters and high stigma costs cheaters are stigmatised. But my interest here is in the dynamics of stigma costs rather than in the description of static coordination games. The costs of being stigmatised are born in the future as well as today. Accounting for the future requires the consideration of stigma cost dynamics.

Concept of Social Exclusion and Social Inclusion

Social exclusion is the denial of equal opportunities imposed by certain groups of society up on others which leads to inability of an individual to participate in the basic political, economic and social functioning of the society. Two defining characteristics of exclusion are particularly relevant, namely, the deprivation caused through exclusion (or denial of equal opportunity) in multiples spheres—showing its multidimensionality. Second feature is that, it is embedded in the societal relations, and societal institutions— the process through which individuals or groups are wholly or partially excluded from full participation in the society in which they live (*Arjan Hann* 1997).

The developments in social science literature indeed enable to comprehend the meanings and manifestations of the concept of social exclusion, and its applicability to caste and ethnicity-based exclusion in India. The manner in which it has been developed in social science literature, the concept of social exclusion, thus, essentially refers to the processes through which groups are wholly, or partially, excluded from full participation in the society in which they live. It emphasises on two crucial dimensions involving the notion of exclusion, namely the 'societal institutions' (of exclusion), and their 'outcome' (in terms of deprivation).

Amartya Sen draws attention to various meanings and dimensions of the concept of social exclusion (*Sen* 2000).

The term social exclusion has its origins in Lenoir (1974; *see also Lenoir*, 1989). Lenoir, then Secretaries allocation Social in the Chirac government, referred to the excluded as consisting not only of the poor but of a wide variety of people, namely the social misfits. The meaning of the term evolved and expanded in the following years to include all individuals and groups that are wholly or partly prevented from participation in their society and in various aspects of cultural and community life.

Social exclusion is of increasing interest because it has gained a primary role in official documents and in the political debate in Europe and, more recently, in Australia, Canada and the United States. In the Treaty of Amsterdam, signed in 1997, the European Union included the reduction of social exclusion among its objectives. During the Lisbon European Council of March 2000, the Union formulated the goal "to become the most competitive dynamic knowledge-based economy in the world capable of sustainable economic growth with more and better jobs and greater social cohesion" (*European Council,* 2000). Clearly, achieving this goal involves the design of policies aimed at combating social exclusion. Both providing a rigorous conceptual foundation and giving some guidance as to the application of the concepts suggested here are of importance because of the public-policy relevance of the issue.

We are not the first to propose a measure of social exclusion. Several attempts have already been made by scholars in various subdisciplines of the social sciences; see, for example, Burchardt, Le Grand and Piachaud (1999), Bradshaw, Williams, Levitas, Pantazis, Patsios, Townsend, Gordon and Middleton (2000), Whclan, Layte and Ma^ýtre (2001), Tsakloglou and Papadopoulos (2002), Chakravarty and D'Ambrosio (2003) and Poggi (2003). As is the case for Chakravarty and D'Ambrosio (2003), we employ the axiomatic method and, to the best of our knowledge, theirs is the only other paper based on it. While their approach and ours exhibit some similarities in the basic setup we use, there are substantial differences in how aspects of social exclusion are taken into consideration. Consequently, the measures we characterise here are very different from those proposed in their contribution.

Social exclusion has received a considerable amount of attention among social scientists discussing the attributes, differences and novelties of it with respect to more traditional concepts such as income poverty, multidimensional poverty and inequality. See, for example, Duffy (1995), Room (1995), Atkinson (1998), Klasen (1998), Rowntree Foundation (1998), Mejer (2000), Sen (2000), Atkinson, Cantillon, Marlier and Nolan (2002), just to mention a few. This paper has a different focus with respect to these earlier contributions: we do not discuss in depth the vagueness of the concept and its characteristics, but our theoretical contribution takes for granted the elements characterising social exclusion that resulted from these debates, and build on those proposing a measure of the phenomenon. At the same time our empirical contribution in calculating the measure takes for granted the variables that Eurostat (2000) deemed appropriate to measure social exclusion in EU member states.

The most fundamental elements identifying the notion of social exclusion are multidimensional functioning failure, relativity and dynamic considerations. Social exclusion is a multi-dimensional concept that covers economic, social and political aspects: it deals with the failure to attain adequate levels of various functionings (*Sen*, 1985) that are deemed valuable in the society under analysis.

The relativity element of social exclusion makes the latter closely related to the concept of deprivation. Runciman (1966) formulates the idea that a person's feeling of deprivation in a society arises out of comparing its situation with those who are better off: "The magnitude of a relative deprivation is the extent of the difference between the desired situation and that of the person desiring it" (*Runciman,* 1966, p.10). This intuition was used by Sen (1976), Yitzhaki (1979) and others to obtain measures of deprivation with income as the relevant variable. In this paper we extend the framework established in the earlier literature.

While the concept of deprivation is usually treated as a static concept, social exclusion has important dynamic aspects: an individual can become socially excluded if its condition of deprivation is persistent or worsens over time. Therefore, the measurement of social exclusion requires the inclusion of time as an important variable (*see also Atkinson,* 1998). Indeed, our distinction between deprivation and social exclusion is captured by this temporal aspect. An individual experiences a higher degree of social exclusion in situations where deprivation is present in consecutive periods as compared to equal levels of deprivation interrupted by periods without deprivation. It is important to note.

METHOD OF STUDY

To facilitate the scientific study and to define the scope of the study the following objectives are farmed.

Objectives

1. To review the Tribal Development Programmes in India;
2. To portray the socio-economic status of the Yerukula community;
3. To examine the change and continuity in livelihood opportunities; levels of education; and access to health care; and
4. To analyse the process of social exclusion and social inclusion resulting in social transformation.

Universe

The universe of the study is Rayalaseema region of Andhra Pradesh. Rayalaseema region comprises four districts *viz.,* Anantapur, Chittor, Kadapa and Kurnool districts. In the Rayalaseema region Yerukula Tribe population is more in the districts of Anantapur and Kurnool districts (33,259 and 24,174 respectively 1991 censes).

Study Sample

A multistage random sampling technique was adopted to draw a representative study sample. At the outset, based on Yerukula tribe population concentration, two districts were chosen. These were Anantapur and Kurnool districts. In the second stage 10 per cent of Revenue mandals (With Yerukulas tribe concentration) from each of the selected districts and 10 per cent of Revenue villages from each of the selected mandals were selected. From each of the selected habitations, 10 per cent of the Yerukula households were selected randomly. Thus, from Anantapur eight habitations of which two urban centers, three semi-urban centers three rural habitations were selected. Similarly one urban center, four semi-urban centers four rural centers from Kurnool district was selected. Our study sample constitutes 300 Yerukula households. The sample comprises 85 urban households, 135 semi-urban households and 80 rural households spread in Kurnool and Anantapur districts of Rayalaseema Region of Andhra Pradesh.

TOOLS OF DATA COLLECTION

The data was collected from both primary and secondary sources. The primary data was collected by administering structured Interview schedule.

The secondary data has been collected from the office of the district Tribal Welfare Office, Kurnool and Anantapur district, Integrated Tribal Development Agency (ITDA) Sreesailam and Tribal Cultural and Research Institute (TCRTI) Hyderabad. National Institute of Rural Development (NIRD) Hyderabad. Indian Council of Social Science Research (ICSSR) Hyderabad.

ANALYSIS OF DATA

The analysis is made with reference to four generations *viz;* Grandfather (G_1), Father (G_2), Respondent (G_3) and Respondent son (G_4) period. The approximate time period of the four generations refer to 1930<for G_1; 1950< for G_2; 1970< for $G_{3;}$ and 1990< for G_4 generations. The data and information gathered was analysed and presented in simple table forms for a clear understanding. The data proposes to make use of both qualitative and quantitative techniques in the analysis of data. Changes in livelihood was analysed by inter-generational and intra-generational occupational mobility and by employing index of dissimilarity. Similarly the levels of living was assessed by employing specially constructed indexes of standard of living, quality of life and social well-being the details are explained in relevant sections. Simple statistical tools like percentages and averages are used in analysing the data. The study is only explorative and descriptive and does not attempt to calculate the rates or ratios or any projections.

SCHEME OF THE STUDY

The present study is divided into *five* chapters. The chapter scheme is as follows.

Chapter I : The *first* chapter covers the introductory part of the study giving the details of the scope of the study and the objectives of the study, conceptual clarifications and review of literature, methodology of the study.

Chapter II : The *second* chapter gives An Ethnographic profile of Yerukula tribes.

Chapter III : The *third* chapter deals with the Profile of Anantapur and Kurnool district, Socio-economic conditions of the Yerukulas.

Chapter IV : The *fourth* chapter presents the analysis and discussion of social exclusion and inclusion process resulting social transformation with reference to livelihood opportunities, levels of education, and access to health care, social participation

Chapter V : The *fifth* chapter summarizes the discussions and the findings of this study.

REFERENCES

Acz'el, J., 1966, *Lectures on Functional Equations and Their Applications, Academic* Press, New York.

Akerlof, G.A. (1997), "Social Distance and Social Decision," *Econometrica,* 65, 1005–1027.

Atkinson, A.B. (1970), "On the Measurement of Inequality," *Journal of Economic Theory,* 2, 244–263.

Atkinson, A.B. (1998), "Social Exclusion, Poverty and Unemployment," in: A.B. Atkinson and J. Hills (eds.), *Exclusion, Employment and Opportunity,* CASE/4, Centre for Analysis of Social Exclusion, London School of Economics, 1–20.

Bradshaw, J., J. Williams, R. Levitas, C. Pantazis, D. Patsios, P. Townsend, D. Gordon and S. Middleton (2000), "The Relationship between Poverty and Social Exclusion in Britain," Paper presented at the 26th General Conference of the International Association for Research in Income and Wealth, Cracow.

Alam, J.1989: 'Tribal identity in Jharkhand', in P.C.Chatterji(ed): Self Image Identity and Nationality (42-56). Shimla: Indian Institute of Advanced Study.

Arnold, D.1982. : 'Rebellious Hillman: Gudem—Rampa Rising 1839-1924', In Ranjit Guha (ed): Subaltern Studies I. Delhi: Oxford University Press.

Belshaw, Cyrill S. 1972. 'Development: The Contribution of Anthropology', *International Social Science Journal,* 24(6): 41-65. 1977. 'The contribution of Anthropologist to Development', in H.M.Mathur (ed): Anthropology in Development Process (45-62). New Delhi: Vikas Publishing House.

Bhattacharjee, S.R.1989. Tribal Insurgency in Tripura: A Study in the Exploration of Causes. New Delhi: Inter-India Publications.

Bose, A. 1990. Tribal Demography and Development in North-Eastern India. Tiplut Nongbri and Delhi: B.R.Publishing Corporation.

Bose, N.K.1941. 'The Hindu Method of Tribal Absorption', Science and Culture, (7): 188-94.

Brass, P.1991. Ethnicity and Nationalism: Theory and Comparison. New Delhi: Sage Publications.

Burman, Roy. B.K. 1972. 'Integrated Area Approach to the Problems of the Hill Tribes of North-east India ', in K.S.Singh (ed): The Tribal Situation in India (67-102). Shimla: Indian Institute of Advanced Study.

Burman, Roy.B.K.1986. Challenges of Development and Tribal Women in India. Udaipur: M.L.V.Tribal Research and Training Institute.

Burchardt, T., J. Le Grand and D. Piachaud (1999) "Social Exclusion in Britain 1991- 1995," *Social Policy and Administration,* 33, 227–244.

Blume, L. E. (1993): "The Statistical Mechanics of Strategic Interaction," *Games and Economic Behaviour,* 4, 387–424.

Chakravarty, S.R. and C. D'Ambrosio (2003), "The Measurement of Social Exclusion," *Discussion Paper,* DIW Berlin.

Chaube, S.C.1973. Hill Politics in North-east India. New Delhi: Orient Longman.

Chaudhuri, B. (ed).1982 'Introduction', in Buddhadeb Chaudhuri (ed): Tribal Development in India (XVII-XXXVI). New Delhi: Inter-India Publications.

Chaudhuri, B. 1992. Ethnopoitics and Identity Crisis. Delhi: Inter India Publications.

Danda, A.K.1973. Tribal Economy and Their Transformation. New Delhi: I.C.S.S.R.

Data, P.S.1993. Autonomy Movements in Assam. Delhi: Omsons Publishers.

Deniroff, R. 1974. The Sociology of Dissent. New York: Hardcourth Bruce Serge Ja Voinovich.

Dommen, A.G.1967. 'Separatist tendencies in Eastern India ', Asian Survey, 7 (10): 726-39.

Dubey, S.M.1982. 'Inter-ethnic alliance, tribal movements and integration in North-east India', in K.S.Singh (ed): Tribal Movements in India, Vol.I (8-19). New Delhi: Manohar.

Dutta, L. 1985. 'Violence in India: The Case of Naga National Movement', Economic and Political Weekly, 16(24): 1053-55.

Duyker, E. 1987. Tribal Guerillas: The Santals of West Bengal and the Naxalite Movement. Delhi: Oxford University Press.

Duclos, J.-Y., J.-M. Esteban and D. Ray (2004), "Polarisation: Concepts, Measurement, Estimation," *Econometrica,* 72, 1737–1772.

Duffy, K. (1995), "Social Exclusion and Human Dignity in Europe," Council of Europe, Strasbourg.

Ebert, U. (1987), "Size and Distribution of Incomes as Determinants of Social Welfare," *Journal of Economic Theory,* 41, 23–33.

Ebert, U. and P. Moyes (2000), "An Axiomatic Characterisation of Yitzhaki's Index of Individual Deprivation," *Economics Letters,* 68, 263–270.

Esteban, J.-M. and D. Ray (1994), "On the Measurement of Polarisation," *Econometrica,* 62, 819–851.

Esteban, J.-M. and D. Ray (1999), "Conflict and Distribution," *Journal of Economic Theory,* 87, 379–415.

European Council (2000), "Presidency Conclusions," Lisbon European Council of 23 and 24 March 2000.

Eurostat (2000), "European Social Statistics. Income, Poverty and Social Exclusion," THEME 3, Population and Social Conditions, Luxembourg.

Fields, G.S. and E.A. Ok (1999), "The Measurement of Income Mobility: An Introduction to the Literature," in J. Silber (ed.), *Handbook of Income Inequality Measurement,* Kluwer, Dordrecht, 557–596.

Fuchs, S. 1965. Rebellions Prophet: A Study of Messianic Movements in India Bombay.

Gough, K. 1979. 'Indian Peasant Uprisings', in A.R.Desai (ed): *Peasant Struggles in India* (85-126). Bombay: Oxford University Press.

Guha, A.1979. 'Great Nationalism, Little Nationalism and Problem of Integration: A Tentative View', *Economic and Political Weekly,* 14(7-8):455-78.

Guha, R.1989a. The Unquiet Wood: Ecological Change and Peasant Resistance in Himalaya. Delhi: Oxford University Press.

Guha, R. 1989b. 'Saboteurs in the Forest: Colonialism and Peasant Resistance in the Indian Himalaya', in Forrest D.Colburn (ed): Everyday Forms of Peasant Resistance. New Delhi: M.E.Sharpe.

Guha, Ranajit. 1983. Elementary Aspects of Peasant Insurgency in Colonial India. Delhi: Oxford University Press.

Hussain, M. 1987. 'Tribal Movements for an Autonomous State in Assam', *Economic and Political Weekly,* 32(3):1329-32.

Imchen, C.L. (1990). 'Issues in Tribal Development', in Ashis Bose, Tiplut Nongbri and Niklesh Kumar (ed): *Tribal Demography and Development In North-eastern India* (40-46). Delhi: B.R. Publishing Corporation.

Karma, M.N. 1998. Social Movements in North-east India. New Delhi: Indus Publishing Company

Klasen, S. (1998), "Social Exclusion and Children in OECD Countries: Some Conceptual Issues," Centre for Educational Research and Innovation, OECD.

Kolm, S.-C. (1969), "The Optimal Production of Social Justice," in J. Margolis and S. Guitton (eds.), *Public Economics,* Macmillan, London, 45–200.

Kandori, M., G. Mailath, and R. Rob (1993): "Learning, Mutation and Long Run Equilibrium in Games," *Econometrica*, 61, 29–56.

Lenoir, R. (1974/1989), Les Exclus: Un Francais sur Dix, Editions du Seuil, Paris.

Link, B. G., and J. C. Phelan (2001): "Conceptualising Stigma," *Annual Review of Sociology,* 27, 363–85.

Mejer, L. (2000), "Statistics on Social Exclusion: The EU Methodological Approach," *Eurostat,* Unit E2 Living Conditions.

Mahpatra, L.K. 1972. 'Social Movements Among Tribes of India', in K.S.Singh (ed): *The Tribal Situation in India* (371-81). Shimla: Indian Institute of Advanced Study.

Nag, C.R. 1993. Mizo Society in Transition. New Delhi: Vikas Publishing House.

Navalalkha, S. (1959). 'The Authority Structure Among the Bhumji and the Bhils: A Study of Historic Causations', The *Eastern Anthropologist,* 13(1): 27-40.

Nuthara, C. 1996. Mizoram: Society and Polity. New Delhi: Indus Publishing Company.

Oommen, T.K. 1981. 'Social Movements, National Crisis and Social Change—the Indian Situation', *NERC Bi-Annual Journal of Social Sciences,* 1:1-17.

Oommen, T.K. 1990. Protest and Change: Studies in Social Movements. New Delhi: Sage Publications.

Pathy, J. 1998. 'Impact of Development Projects on Tribals', in Vidut Joshi (ed): *Tribal Situation in India: Issues in Development* (275-86). New Delhi: Rawat Publications.

Paul, M.C. 1989. Dimensions of Tribal Movements in India: A Study of Udayachal in Assam Valley. New Delhi: Inter-India Publications.

Pratap, D.R. 1982. 'Approach to Tribal Development', in Buddadeb Chaudhury (ed): Tribal Development in India. New Delhi: Inter India Publication.

Planning Commission Report on Welfare of SC/ST and Other BCs, Government of India, New Delhi. 2000-02.

Poggi, A. (2003), "Does Persistence of Social Exclusion Exist in Spain?" *Working Paper* 03-08, Department of Applied Economics, and Universidad Autonomy de Barcelona.

Raghaviah, V. 1979. 'Tribal Revolts in Chronological Order: 1778 to 1971', in A.R. Desai (ed): *Peasant Struggles in India* (23-27). Bombay: Oxford University Press.

Rao, M.S.A. (ed). 1979. Social Movements in India, Vol.1. New Delhi: Manohar Publications.

Ray, A. 1982. Mizoram: Dynamics of Change. Calcutta: Pearl Publishers.

Rotter-Hogan, e. 1982. 'Insurrection or Ostracism: A Study of Santal Rebellion of 1855', *Contributions to Indian Sociology*, 16(1): 79-96.

Room, G. (1995), *Beyond the Threshold: The Measurement and Analysis of Social Exclusion,* Policy Press, Bristol.

Rowntree Foundation (1998), "The Report of Key Indicators of Poverty and Social Exclusion," available at www.parliament.the-stationery-office.co.uk.

Runciman, W.G. (1966), *Relative Deprivation and Social Justice,* Routledge, London.

Sen, A.K. (1973), *On Economic Inequality,* Oxford University Press, Oxford.

Sen,A.K. (1976), "Poverty: An Ordinal Approach to Measurement," *Econometrica,* 44, 219–231.

Sen, A.K. (1985), *Commodities and Capabilities,* North Holland, Amsterdam.

Sen, A.K. (1998), "Social Exclusion and Economic Measurement," paper presented at the 25th General Conference of the International Association for Research in Income and Wealth, Cambridge.

Sareen, H.K. 1980. Insurgency in North-East: a Study of Sino-American Role. New Delhi; Sterling Publishers.

Sen, J. 1969. 'The Jharkhand Movement' *Seminar on the Tribal Situation in India.*

Sengupta, N. 1980. 'Caste and Tribals in Jharkandh', *Economic and Political Weekly,* 15(14): 664-71.

Sharma, K.L.1986. *Caste Class and Social Movements.* Jaipur: Rawat Publications.

Singh, B. 1982(ed). Steps Towards Tribal Development. The Third Step: Training of Trainers in Tribal Development Administration. Delhi: Department of Personal Administration, Government of India.

Singh, K.S. 1977. 'From Ethnicity to Regionalism: A Study of Tribal Politics and Movements in Chotanagpur from 1900 to 1975', in S.C. Malik (ed): Dissent, Protest and Reform in Indian Civilisation (317-43). Shimla: Indian Institute of Advanced Study.

Singh, K.S. 1982. *Tribal Movements in India,* Vol.1. New Delhi: Manohar Publications.

Singh, K.S. 1983a. 'Introduction', in K.S.Singh (ed): *Tribal Movements in India,* Vol. 2. New Delhi: Manohar Publications.

Singh, K.S. 1983c. 'The Tribal Autonomy Movements in Chhotanagpur', in K.S.Singh (ed): *Tribal Movements in India,* Vol. 2. New Delhi: Manohar Publications.

Singh, K.S. 2002. 'Tribal Autonomy Movements in Chhotanagpur', in Ghanshaym Shah (ed): Social Movements and the State (267-92). New Delhi: Sage Publications.

Singh, R. 2001. Social Movements, Old and New: A Post-Modernist Critique. New Delhi: Sage Publications.

Singh, S. 2002. 'Tribal Solidarity Movements in India: A Review', in Ghanshyam Shah (ed): Social Movements and the State (251-66). New Delhi: Sage Publications.

Subba Ramaraju, Sudhakar,C. Developmental Programmes and Social Transformation. Associated Publishers, New Delhi-2006.

Tsakloglou, P. and F. Papadopoulos (2002), "Identifying Population Groups at High Risk of Social Exclusion: Evidence from the ECHP," in: R.J.A. Muffels, P. Tsakloglou and D.G. Mayes (eds.), *Social Exclusion in European Welfare States,* Edward Elgar, Cheltenham, Chapter 6.

Thakur, A. 2001. Tribal Development and Its Paradoxes. New Delhi: Authors Press.

Thorat, Sukhadeo (1999), 'Social Security in Unorganised Sector, How Secure are the Scheduled Caste? Special Issue', *Indian Journal of Labour Economic*, September.

Umamohan, C. A.Naganna, Occupational Changes and Mobility: An Intra-Generational Study of Yerukulas in Rayalaseema Region of AP. National Seminar on 3rd and 4th November, 2006. Dravidian University, Kuppam.

Upadhaya, A. 1980b. 'Class struggle in Rural Maharashtra, India: Toward a New Perspective', The Journal of Peasant Studies, vii (2):46-62.

Unpublished Monograph of TCRTI, Government of Andhra Pradesh. 2000. and Rural Household Healthcare Needs and Availability, 1992.

Vidyarthi, L.P. 1977. The Tribal Culture of India. Delhi: Concept Publishing Company.

Vidyarthi, L.P. 1981. Tribal Development and Its Administration. New Delhi: Concept Publishing House.

UK House of Commons (1999), "Poverty and Social Exclusion (National Strategy) Bill," available at www.parliament.the-stationery-office.co.uk.

Wang, Y.-Q. and K.-Y. Tsui (2000), "Polarisation Orderings and New Classes of Polarisation Indices," *Journal of Public Economic Theory,* 2, 349–363.

Whelan, C.T., R. Layte and B. Maitre (1999), "Persistent Deprivation in the European Union," *Working Paper No. 23,* European Panel Analysis Group.

Wolf son, M.C. (1994), "When Inequalities Diverge," *American Economic Review,* 84, 353–358.

Weiner, M. 1978. Sons of the Soil: Migration and Ethnic Conflict in India. New Jersey: Princeton University Press.

Yitzhaki, S. (1979), "Relative Deprivation and the Gini Coefficient," *Quarterly Journal of Economics,* 93, 321–324.

Young, H. P. (1993): "The Evolution of Conventions," *Econometrica,* 61, 5784.

Chapter 2

The Yerukula
An Ethnographic Profile

INTRODUCTION

Among the South Indian Tribes, the Yerukalas occupy an important place. They are one of the largest tribes of Andhra Pradesh. They also comprise one of the most ancient tribes. The great Indian epic *Mahabharata* has mentioned about the Yerukalas as adept in archery.

They are found in the vast areas extending from the gorges of the Godavari in the North to the plains of the river Pinakini in the South. These people are found chiefly in Kurnool. Guntur, Krishna, Prakasam, Cuddapah, Anantapur, East Godavari, West Godavari, Chittoor and Nellore district of Andhra Pradesh.

The Yerukalas, in fact, are found throughout the erstwhile Madras Presidency, though called by a different name, as Koravas. As railways spread all over the country, they could spread all over the country in different names.

POPULATION

The total population of Andhra Pradesh, as per the 2001 Census, is 76,210,007.Of which, 5,024,104 (6.6 per cent) are Scheduled Tribes (STs). The ST population constitutes 6 per cent of the country's ST population. The Scheduled Castes and Scheduled Tribes Orders (Amendment) Act, 1976 have notified 33 STs in the state. (Table 2.1)

Table 2.1. Distribution of Yerukula Population in Andhra Pradesh

Sl. No.	Year	All Tribes in Andhra Pradesh	Yerukulas	% to Total tribal poulalation to Andhra Pradesh
1	1961	1324370	128024	9.6
2	1971	1657657	162560	9.8
3	1981	3176001	300557	9.4
4	1991	4199481	387898	9.2
5	2001	5024104	437459	8.7

Source: 1. Office of the Registrar General, India, 2001.
2. Census of India, 2001.

Yerukulas are mostly found in the plain areas of Andhra Pradesh and they live in traditionally dome shaped huts made out of bamboo poles and palmary leaves. There are no walls in this type of houses. The roofs made out of palmary leaves firmly stitched from top to the ground level on the bamboo framework. The narrow openings of the houses are covered with small wattles made out of bamboo sticks whenever they leave huts. The settlements of Yerukulas are generally found in the outskirts of the villages or towns near the canals or other water resources in order to rear their pigs. They also settle-down where raw material especially dates trees and bamboos are available for making baskets.

Yeru is connected with erra, meaning red. Yerukalavandlu means, sooth Sayers, fortune-tellers. Gustav Oppert suggests that this word is the origin of Yerukula. Francis writes of them as: A gypsy tribe found all over the Tamil Country, but chiefly in Kurnool, Salem, Coimbatore and South Arcot.

ETYMOLOGY

Etymologically, the word "Yerukulas" is derived from the Telugu word Yeruka *which* means presence. The word *Yerukula* is used by the people of Coastal Andhra and Telangana.

Several derivations of Yerukalas have been proposed by many sociologists. Yeru is connected with erra, meaning red. Yerukalavandlu means, sooth Sayers, fortune-tellers. Gustav Oppert suggests that this word is the origin of Yerukula.

About the Yerukalas of the Godavari district, Rev. J. Cain, (1880: IX) stated: Among themselves they call each other Kuluvaru, but the Telugu people call them Erakavaru or Erakalavaru and their name has been derived from the Telugu word Eruka, which means knowledge or acquaintance, as they are great fortune-tellers.

Name

The tribe goes by different names in different localities. It is known as Korava from the extreme south to the north of the North Arcot district. In Mysore, it is called Koracha, and in Rayalaseema they become Yerukula or Yerukula. Some Koravas pass for Vellalas, and call themselves Agambadia Vellalas with the title Pillai. Others call themselves Pillai, Kavaraj, Idiyan, Reddy etc. (*Thurston, Edgar;* 1909:439).

Koravas have been treated as being the same as Yerukulas. The Yerukulas and Koravas have identity with each other. The appellation Koracha or Korcha appears to be of a later date than Korava and said to be derived from the Hindustani Kory (sly), korrinigga (sly look) becoming corrupted into Korcha.

Language

They always speak themselves as Kurru. Their language is peculiar and seems to be distinctly of a Tamil origin. They are however conversant with Tamil, Telugu and Kannada dialects which are spoken according to the locality they visit. They use slang expressions which are perfectly unintelligible to the outsiders.

Clan and Gothra

The Yerukula tribe divided into a number of functional and endogamous sub-divisions and each such sub-division is named after the commodity which they traded in and the occupation they adopted. The endogamous occupattional sub-divisions are 1. *Dabba Yerukula* (those who make baskets from split bamboo), 2. *Yeethapulla* (date twins) Yerukula (those make baskets from wild date leaves), 3. *Kunchapuri Yerukula* (those who make weaver's combs), 4. *Prikimuggula Yerukula* (sooth sayers and beggars), 5. *Karivepaku Yerukula* (Hawkers of Curry leaves), and 5. *Uppu Yerukula* (salt hawkers).

Each sub-division is divided into four phratries *viz.;* Sathupadi, Kavadi, Manupati and Mendraguthi. The first two phratries *viz.;* Sathuapadi and Kavadi are considered to be superior to the other two. Each phratry is further sub-divided into a number of exogenous intiperlu (Sure names), some of the intiperlu are Kumbha, Mogili, Katta Devara, Sreerama, Palaparthi, Meda etc. Endogamy at community level and exogamy at Phratry and Intiperlu level are observed.

Their gotras or clans or divisions are found in considerable number and or in accordance with their gradation. They are Sathepati, Kavadi, Mnapatti, and Mendragutti. These are all corrupted Tamil words: 1. Sathepathi is a corruption of Sathupadi which mans adorning a Hindu deity with flowers and jewels and vestments; 2. Kavadi shortly pronounced is kavadi, meaning a pole carried on the shoulders, with two basket pendants hanging from both its ends in which are kept the offerings for a deity or temple; 3. Manapati is a corruption of manpadi, means singing in praise of God, when He is worshipped in a temple; 4. Mendragutti is a corruption of enrikutti, which means stitching a pair of shoes and presenting it to the temple, a custom still prevalent at Tirupati, at Sri Venkateswara shrine and others.

Of these four major divisions, the first two are considered superior to the other two, a Kavadi man being styled pothuvadu (male) and a Sathepati women, pente (female), meaning thereby in the Telugu language that they are endogamous with a preference to Kavadi men and are more entitled to marry Sathepati women than Sathepati men. But this custom gradually died down.

They have innumerable family or house names, such as Wayyalu, Bandi, Ambojala, Avula, Mekala, Merameai, Mote, Devara, Bochu, Malle, Kampa, Gajjala, Pula, Samudrala and soon consequent on some peculiar incidents in their families.

They were also subdivided into different groups in different provinces according to their professions and means of livelihood.

Though these gotras or house names are found in every one of them, some of these sub-divisions are exogamous; but in their common pursuit of robbery, they are indistinguishable. A gang of Koravas in Southern India embraced Islam and thereafter they are being called as Mohammedan Koravas. Some Yerukalas, who have become educated and respectable members of society, call themselves as Balijas or Naidus to get a respectable place.

Two subdivisions of Yerukalas, Kavadi and Wooyaloo, do not inter-dine or inter-marry amonst themselves. As has been learnt from the interviews, they claim their origin from some important incidents in their family.

Captain Harvey mentioned about five classes of the Kaikaries in his report, *viz.,* Gam Kaikaries, Koonchee Kaikaries, Koot Kaikaries, Sursal Kaikaries and Ran Kaikaries.

The Yerukulas, as indicated earlier, are called differently in different localities and has assumed various names, according to their settlement names, in different parts of India, According to their profession and ostensible means of livelihood, they are again divided into subdivisions in different provinces, *e.g.,*

1. Uppa Koravas (salt-sellers); 2. Karuvepaei Koravas (a kind of leaf used to add favour to the preparation of food); 3. Thabbai koravas (sellers of bamboo talties,

mats, baskets, ropes, ropenets, strings and granaries); 4. Kavalkar Koravas (watchmen); 5. Pachakutti or Grade Koravas; 6. Kallu Koravas or men-ding stones and working Wadde Yerukulas on roads by carrying stones and mud); 7. Gadepatti Kaikaries (basket making); 8. Konche Koravas (to make brushes for sale); 9. Koot Kaikaries koot means dancing – so they live by prostitution); 10. Pam Kaikaries (exhibit serpents from door to door and beg); 11. Bhajantree Koravas (attend marriages and other feasts with their coarse and crude music and get remuneration).

Family and Marriage

Family is an important segment in the social structure of any community of people. In sociological terms, the word 'family' is used to connote, 1. The household 2. The body of persons living under an umbrella of one manager (this including parents, children) 3. Kinship among them 4. Existence of one common ancestor.

The type of family among Yerukula tribe is usually nuclear. Descent is patrilineal, residence is patrilocal and authority is partriarchal. The son could live away from the joint family, but share could not be claimed from his paternal property during his father's life time. If the father dies leaving behind a number of children, his surviving brothers would come to the rescue of the minor children. Children so reared would support their uncles during their old age as a mark of gratitude. Nuclear family system has stepped in the life style in the recent times.

Among the Yerukalas, a girl, after marriage, joins her husband. So the family system is patriarchal. However, woman occupies a very important place in the tribe, not only as mother but as the guardian of all properties. They lead a life separated from all others, and are rigid and tenacious in following their customs and rules. They are particular about the reputation of their women and consider it a serious offence if a woman returns home after dusk without an escort.

The son could live away from the joint family, but share could not be claimed from his paternal property during his father's life time. If the father dies leaving behind a number of children, his surviving brothers would come to the rescue of the minor children. Children so reared would support their uncles during their old age as a mark of gratitude. Nuclear family system has stepped into their life style in the recent times.

In Yerukula society, a family is a corporate group acting together to meet their common purposes. The members of Yerukula tribe, share social, economic and religious rituals and also learn the basic things of culture. They also share their personal achievements with their families. Parthasarathy states, (1988): A family is not only a reproductive unit but a socialising agency. Duties rights and privileges of social life of individual are tied with kinship relationships. Anthropologists classify the decent rules as the cognatic decent rules applied to both the genders. Unilineal rules accomplish the same results, but they restrict parental links exclusively to one gender. In Yerukula community patrilineality exists instead of matrilineality.

The social structure of Yerukulas is based upon patriarchal system, but there is a perfect understanding between husband and wife.

Family is an important segment in the social structure of any community of people. In sociological terms, the word 'family' is used to connote, 1. The household 2. The body of persons living under an umbrella of one manager (this including parents, children) 3. Kinship among them 4. Existence of one common ancestor.

The type of family among Yerukula tribe is usually nuclear. Descent is patrilineal, residence is patrilocal and authority is partriarchal. The son could live away from the joint family, but share could not be claimed from his paternal property during his father's life time. If the father dies leaving behind a number of children, his surviving brothers would come to the rescue of the minor children. Children so reared would support their uncles during their old age as a mark of gratitude. Nuclear family system has stepped in the life style in the recent times.

In Yerukula society, a family is a corporate group acting together to meet their common purposes. The members of Yerukula tribe, share social, economic and religious rituals and also learn the basic things of culture. They also share their personal achievements with their families. Parthasarathy states, (1988): A family is not only a reproductive unit but a socializing agency. Duties rights and privileges of social life of individual are tied with kinship relationships. Anthropologists classify the decent rules as the cognatic decent rules applied to both the genders. Unilineal rules accomplish the same results, but they restrict parental links exclusively to one gender. In Yerukula community patrilineality exists instead of matrilineality.

Among the Yerukalas, a girl, after marriage, joins her husband. So the family system is patriarchal. However, woman occupies a very important place in the tribe, not only as mother but as the guardian of all properties. They lead a life separated from all others, and are rigid and tenacious in following their customs and rules. They are particular about the reputation of their women and consider it a serious offense if a woman returns home after dusk without an escort.

The son could live away from the joint family, but share could not be claimed from his paternal property during his father's life time. If the father dies leaving behind a number of children, his surviving brothers would come to the rescue of the minor children. Children so reared would support their uncles during their old age as a mark of gratitude. Nuclear family system has stepped into their life style in the recent times.

The type of marriage that exists among the Yerukalas is polygamy. A man can marry any number of women. But this idea is getting weaker and weaker everyday and now a man is hesitant to take more than one wife, generally. Thus, they are favouring monogamy. Though they observe no caste differences in eating or drinking, they have their own reservations in point of marriage. Their marriages are exogamous. They freely admit other caste women into theirs, except those of the lowest order, such as, Malas, Madigas and the like. A marriage is generally negotiated between the parents of the bridegroom and the bride and the former promise to pay a voli or 'bride-price' (sullaponnu) of 20 pagodas for the first marriage and 2 pagodas for the re-marriage of man or a woman (one pagoda means Rs.3.50). The ceremony is very simple. The marriage bond is considered inviolable among the members of the tribe. After the betrothal ceremony, the parents of the girl should, on no account, break the marriage proposal.

Marriage ceremony is known as kannalam, in their language. The marriageable age of a girl is 14-16 years and for the boy it is 18-20 years. The father of the boy along with some elders of the community, meets the father of the boy along with some elders of the community, meets the father of the girl. After this, a day is fixed for the performance of a gumadu (betrothal) ceremony. On the fixed day, these elders proceed with a new mat and spread it in front of the house. The girl's father and the members of the kulapanchayat sit on the mat and decide the bride-price. Liquor is served depending upon the financial position of the bride-groom's father. Then they fix the date of the marriage.

Now-a-days the performance of the marriage takes place generally in the houses, rarely nearest temple. Brahmin pujari perform the ceremony.

Marriage is celebrated for three days at the bride's house. First day is known as gajumetti (angle and toe-ring). The bride has to wear the bangles and the bridegroom has to wear the toe-ring. Kankanams are tied to the wrists of the couple. Second day's ceremony is called toorpu vakili (east door). Two temporary huts are constructed in front of the bride's house and their doors are directed towards East. Left hut is allotted to the bride and right to the groom. In bride's hut they keep lighted oil lamp, one new bamboo basket and sling. In the groom's hut they keep kalasam (metallic vessel with coconut on top of it). The couple are given oil-bath and dressed in new clothes. They are taken to the marriage huts, amidst the invities and spend the day inside the huts.

The third day ceremony is known as talabalu. The betrothal pair, in front of their allotted huts, are smeared with oil five times and they take oil bath. Then the parents of bride, the father carrying on his head a new pot and mother holding in hand lighted lamps, proceed to the village well. Twig of the papal tree with five off-shots is acquired and placed in the earthen pot filled with water. The lighted oil lamp has to remain until the marriage ceremony is over. Then the couple is seated facing the pot, on a date palm mat spread underneath the bower. The tali (mangala sutra) thread with black beads is tied around the bride's neck. It is followed by talabalu ceremony. A non-vegetarian feast is served along with liquor. The marriage procession takes place in the night. The two huts temporarily erected are removed. According to their customary law, they should not use musical instruments during the marriage ceremony.

The maternal uncle's right to the first daughter is valued at 8 pagodas. Naturally, he becomes the recipient of the bride-price. In case they are poor, at least half of the fixed bride-price must be paid before the ceremony, to enable the girl's father to pay off maternal uncle's share and commence wedding preparations. The balance may be cleared in instalments. Maternal uncle need not return the bride-price in case of bride's death or divorce. If he advances his preferential claim and marries his own sons to his nieces, he may pay as concession only 12 pagodas for the two. If he is not in a position to take the bride as his daughter-in-law, he receives 8 of the 20 pagodas from the girl's parents. Generally, the marriage ceremony (kannalam) is over in one day, but drinking continues for three days at the expense of parents of the couple, if they can afford it. Ordinarily, Hindu marriage traditions are followed. However, in some cases, their conversion to Christianity has its influence on the marriage performance in which case it is solemnised in the Church.

Widow marriages are rampant in Yerukula Community. A woman can marry seven times, provided at the time of every subsequent marriage, her previous husband is not alive or she has been granted separation or divorce from her previous husband by the kulapanchayat. Widow is given new clothing. The person marrying her presents a new saree in front of her house and she wears it. He pays Rs.24 as bride-price to the former father-in-law of his would be a wife.

Child marriages are rare among Yerukulas. Another interesting factor among the Yerukalas is when any man of a gang goes to jail; the wife selects another partner for the period of her husband's absence and goes back to the original husband on his release, with all her children, though they might have been born to her make-shift husband.

There are some drastic rules in the social code of Yerukulas. The Yerukulas can, in no case, marry a woman of any caste or community lower than that of his own. If he does, all the clan members are excommunicated by the kulapanchayat in the presence of all the community members. The man who elopes with a 'low caste' woman must necessarily undergo a process of purification ceremony. After burning his tongue with a gold-piece in the presence of all his tribe, he is re-admitted into the caste. This offence may be committed by a single person, but the entire clan is held responsible for that. Sexual intercourse between the persons of the same sect is a social stigma. That individual has to undergo the same purification ceremony and it is followed by a community dinner. The marriage of that girl would be arranged in order to avoid further complications. If any extra-martial intercourse case happens, and if the girl is caught in the very act, the husband complains about the matter to the kulapanchayat. If the husband is willing to keep his wife with him inspite of this, the culprit is expected to pay a fine of Rs.50 to the kulapanchayat. Otherwise, she has to pay all the expenses of marriage to her husband and Rs.50 as fine to kulapanchayat. The man who is thus involved in adultery receives her as his second wife and the children born to the married husband are to be claimed by him. A man cannot dare to speak ill of any other woman. If a woman is spoken ill of, she reports the matter to the kulapanchayat and immediately the person responsible has to pay a fine Rs.8 as notithappu or talking ill of a lady. This norm is meant to maintain the social status and reverence for the woman in the community.

In Yerukula language divorce is know as rookha perkucodithulu. The divorcees are allowed to remarry. The marriage is an agreement between the kin's persons of both the sides. There are certain conditions prescribed by the kulapanchayat at the time of marriage. Their breach causes for divorce. They are barrenness, laziness, adultery, desertion of a wife after elopement and incurable diseases. Husband's impotence, failure to support the family, cruel treatment is some other important reasons for divorce. The divorce parties may, if they desire, patch up their differences and continue to keep the family ties.

Kulapanchayat is the right full organisation to deal with such cases. In the presence of both the parents, the husband has to give a pot of toddy with betel leaves and supari (nut) along with rooka (25 paisa) to his wife. If the divorce is on account of adultery or desertion by the wife, the new bride-groom has to pay half of the amount of the bride-price and the complete expenditure of marriage to the previous husband.

In case of elopement, the father of the girl summons the kulapanchayat at which the accused is penalised. The man who elopes with the girl is forced to marry her. It is not forbidden, because polygamy is widely practiced and socially sanctioned.

Birth and Death

Immediately after the birth of a baby, they burn incense in front of the house and distribute sweet-meats to the elders of the family. On the ninth day of birth, the ceremony of naming the child takes place. The responsibility of doing this lies with the maternal uncle, who ties a string round the waist of the newly born. The string wearing indicates the entry of a new member into the Yerukula community.

If a wandering Yerukula dies, he is buried without any delay by keeping his had to the north and feet to the south. Hindu customs followed in the disposal of a dead body and the same religious rituals are observed. But some of them also observe the cremation method practiced by Hindus.

Economic Life

The Yerukulas were mainly dependent upon the collection of make baskets with wild date leaves for their livelihood. They used to collect cat, pits, field-rats, goats and sheep, Jackals, serve as items of food for them. They had hardly developed any technique for preservation of food, perhaps it reflected a world view whose perceptual concerned was today and not tomorrow. But this picture of food gathering economy and un-commitment worldview is a partial picture only.

To many Yerukula agriculture is an important occupation such as agricultural labour or petty business. However, they are not skillful in it. paddy is the main corp produced by them. But this depends mainly on a good and timely monsoon. Even while walking, they make ropes, fishing nets and baskets.

Yerukulas deal in salt, tamarind, jaggery; curry leaves (karaveipaku), wandering from place to place and carrying the commodities on back of donkeys or bullocks. The curry leaves called karepaku has been in great demand in Andhra area; so their women folks carry on this brisk trade. In addition, they purchase all kinds of grams at lower rate and sell them at a higher prices.

While doing this, they study the topography of the village and carry on highway robberies and decoities. The Karuvepalli Koravas (Yerukalas) are considered to be the worst type of high way bandits.

The Thabbai and Koodkalte Koravas settle in towns and villages and sell bamboo tails, date-mats, baskets, ropes, rope-nets, slings and granaries.

Generally, they live on the outskirts of the towns and the villages and develop acquaintance with the local bad-hats and goldsmiths.

They are adepts in disposing off stolen properties and help their brethren in this service.

A section of Yerukalas, called Kunchu Yerukulas, gather roots from the forest and make them into nets which are used by weavers. Some of them prepare fine nets for fishing and some make knots with the rope on which the chatties (earthen pots) are kept.

As for the Kavalkar Koravas, (kaval means watching), they are employed as village watchmen; they follow the principle of setting a thief to catch a thief. They are looked after by the villagers for the service rendered by them in keeping watch over the fields. Generally, the Kavalkar Koravas are responsible in tracing out culprits and handing them over to the proper authorities. Shepherds commit thefts in villages and Kavalkars keep watch over them.

Some times, the Yerukalas beg in the villages, taking a monkey or snake with them. They go from house to house and there by eke out their livelihood.

The women earn their living mainly in two ways—one, tattooing and two, fortune-telling. The pictures generally used for tattooing by the Yerukula women are: fish, scorpions, other conventional designs and names. They have skill in drawing these pictures on the skin of the people. This tattooing fetches the women rice instead of money. The fortune-teller is called gadde and fortune-telling as sodi in

Telugu area. These women start with a basket and winnowing with it they shout and proclaim that their ostensible occupation is sooth-saying. While roaming thus, if any body engages them, they study the ingress and egress and other particulars of the house and inform these to their men, who commit theft in those very houses at night. The women invoke the blessings of different goddesses before they proceed to tell fortune. They use a winnowing fan and separate grains of rice from the chaff and put them on the fan. On doing this properly depends whether the prophesy will be good or evil; this is judged from the counting of the grains found on the fan. They carry along with them a basket, winnowing fan, stick and a wicker tray in which cowry shells are embedded in dough of cow-dung mixed with turmeric. Even now, this practice is in vogue in Andhra Pradesh.

Even now their earnings from a particular type of occupation are insufficient, in the large majority of cases, and they are hard put to maintain their families. Therefore, there is a shift towards other occupations, such as agricultural labour or petty business.

To many Yerukalas, agriculture is an important occupation. However, they are not skillful in it. Paddy is the main crop produced by them. But this depends mainly on a good and timely monsoon. Though physically the Yerukalas are a robust people, by habit they are lazy and lethargic.

Yerukalas are not without good or praise worthy qualities of their own. They are clever and skillful. Even while walking, they make ropes, fishing nets and baskets.

As stated before, the primary occupations of Yerukalas of Kaparallatippa and Sitanagaram Settlements are: 1. agriculture; 2 crime; 3.agricultural labour; 4. business; 5. quarrying and 6. Government jobs.

The ex-settlers of the two villages have adopted some other occupations besides their traditional occupation, due to the impact of environmental influences.

It appears that Yerukulas are some what interested in rearing animals like pigs, sheep, goats and some of them are keeping poultry also. Very few Yerukulas are rearing goats and sheep. If the pigs are less in number, they share the living quarters of their hosts.

Kula Panchayat

The culture and social organisation of the Yerukalas is quite different from any other tribe of the country. The code of conduct of every individual is determined and controlled by an organisation called kulapanchayat or caste assembly. They have great respect for the unwritten law or the verdict of kulapanchayat. The caste assembly enforces rigid principles on them. Irrespective of the sect or his position in the society, every Yerukula man sub-ordinates himself to the will of the elders or the leaders of their own tribe. The head of the village is called beromanesam or a big man. The Yerukula leaders decide whether a man is guilty of an allegation or not by dipping the fingers of the accused person in boiling oil or making him pick up a red-hot iron rod or walking through a crackling bed of fire etc. If the accused is injured during such a test, he is adjudged guilty. Though the methods involved here are uncivilised and barbarous, they are very simple and do not have a chance of perjury or impersonation. The beromanesam is selected on account of his age, intelligence and the influence he commands by virtue of love and affection shown to him by the community. The kulapanchayat consists of five persons. People listen to the complaints and then manage to arrive at an unanimous decision. In this connection V. Raghavaiah quotes, (1977:52): Fawcett says that the Kulam or tribal assembly adjudicates claims, inflicts penalties, ejects individuals from the tribe or readmits them there too.

Free drinking of toddy at the expense of the parties happens in every caste assembly. It is the aggrieved party which gives notice to the assembly or the kulam. The disputants join hands, thereby suggesting to the kulam that their dispute should be decided by them. Each pays one rupee. The kulam or the tribe may decided the dispute at once or adjourn it till the next meeting. In the second meeting also they pay one rupee each for toddy. A person, who fails to attend, when the kulam is assembled, has to forego his membership in the tribe. If there is a third party joining the hands, each side pays three rupees and a half for toddy to keep the tribe in good spirits. In the final adjournment, the decision is taken by mans of a test. An equal quality of rice is placed in two pots of equal weight, having an equal quantity of water and an equal quantity of fuel. The judges then satisfy themselves mot carefully as to the quantity, the weight and so on. The water is boiled and the man whose rice boils first is declared to be the winner of the dispute. The loser is to recoup the winner all his expenses. Another method is: picking up a coin from a pot containing boiling oil. The man who picks up without injury is declared winner. The Tamil proverb 'Kuravans justice, the ruin of the family' is quite apt, because it refers to the endless nature of the quarrels and decisions all of which are prolonged. Thus, there are generally three different ways in which Panchayats meet: 1. Caste dinner at which somebody taking advantage of the assembly gets up and gives a complaint; 2. when it is specially summoned by the aggrieved person; 3. when it is definitely summoned to discuss problems of importance.

Beliefs and Festivals

Yerukulas believe in luck and superstitions. It they happen to see any animals whose flesh is edible or a cow or dog cow or dog coming without shaking the ears but shaking the tail, it is considered as good own. In the every Yerukulas house there is Rolu and Rokali for husking the grain. Rolu is made of stone and Rokali is made of wood. They use Chata to clean the rice before cooking. They use baskets of various types, manufactured from the materials abundantly available in the forests. These days they are accustomed to use aluminum and stainless steel vessels. The household implements include Goddali (axe) Sorakathi (axe used for killing and skinning the animals); Para (used for loosening the soil); Pikas (Pick axe); Kodavali (sickle) used for cutting grass and crop; they also use Gurru (Plough with three coulter for the sowing). They are all made of iron.

Yerukulas hear a tiger rearing during April/may, they supposed that the coming year will bring then good rains, harvesting structure in the month of October and continues till December. After threshing operations are over, the food-grains are collected and stored in baskets for further consumption. The baskets are made a bamboo in different sizes. They believe that April to August is the lucky period for marriage.

Yerukulas generally use Pull Goya (A bamboo flute), Burragoya (nagasweram) as musical instruments.

Festivals: Yerukulas worship Hindu gods *i.e.* Vishnu in the form of Lord Venkateswara and his consort, Laxmi, Narasimhaswamy, Nrayanaswamy and Rama. They also worship minor deities like Bhawani, Mahalaxmi, Poleramma, Maremma, Peddamma etc. Pig, Jackal, Crow and other animals and birds are used as offerings for sacrifices to these deities.

It is believed that they have been much influenced by Hindus of the neighbouring villages. They celebrated Hindu festivals such as Sankranthi, Sivarathri, Sreeramanavami, Dasara, Ugadi (Telugu New Year's Day). Few of them celebrate Deepavali festival also. During the Dasara festival, they worship Jammi tree. At the time of worship on the festive occasions, they break new coconuts and Buru incense. On these occasions, they wear new clothes if they can offer; otherwise, they put on washed ones.

Criminality

Hume, in 1855 presented an alternative framework of analysis. He spoke of the good qualities of the members of criminal tribes such as fidelity and courage. He felt the urgent need to assist and reclaim them. He regarded their criminality as the direct consequence of absolute hardship and the intolerant and often brutal attitude of the police. Almost like savages and utterly reckless of their life, they are perpetually goaded into crimes. The moment the police hear of their arrival, they proceed to drive them away, hounding them from village to village with harsh words and beatings (Official Publications, Selection from Records No. XXIII, Act 6, Boureeath Gang Papers, Ioh, V/23/119).

The Woddars and Yerukalas from Guntur and Hyderabad territories caused havoc in Krishna district. In order to curb the activities of the criminals, the then Madras Government decided to declare the above two as criminal tribes. We will now examine the factors responsible for declaring the Yerukulas as a criminal tribe.

The criminal tendency of the Yerukalas is more due to their broken social life, under pressures of economic and territorial displacements, than anything else. They had to move from place to place for getting food and shelter. This displacement affected seriously their old pattern of life leading to maladjustments in society. Secondly, the introduction of railways was a setback to the wee bit trade or business that the Yerukalas were carrying on, though, as stated earlier, it helped their quick movement to and from the places of crime as also in the wide areas of operation. Salt business and selling of curry leaves became too difficult for them, to carry on as before. Thirdly, the general near-famine conditions of the Madras Presidency compelled them to take up criminal activity for subsistence. Fourthly, the adverse climatic conditions and the rise in the prices of essential commodities of life led them to the part of crime. Fifthly, their behavioral patterns, *i.e.,* the easy going ways of life gave them scope to pursue criminal activities. Moreover, they are an intelligent and clever lot, which acted as a favourable point to choose this type of living. Sixthly, the Zamindars and landlords, who were the investors in crime, encouraged them to take up crime for their own selfish ends. Seventhly, some Yerukalas served as intelligent corps (charus) in the services of medieval kingdoms, and later under the Rajas and Zamindars. Also, they were employed in the standing armies of the kings and local chieftains and when the British occupied these areas, the local armies were disbanded and replaced by the British army. Consequently, the Yerukalas lost their means of honest living and took to thieving.

Heredity and environment are the important factors generally considered in deciding about criminality of a person. The C.T. Act criminals, in olden days, were treated as sub-human beings by the then administrators who posed themselves as their saviors and mentors. They were led by a faulty doctrinaire as: (1) once a criminal, ever a criminal; and (2) criminals are born and not made and, therefore, criminality is a hereditary disease. The administrators went so far as to apply the savage law of separating the children of the C.T. Act criminals within the age group 4 to 18 from their irreclaimable parents, so as to keep the children apart from the criminal atmosphere. The harshness of the Act was, however, mitigated to some extent by a few amendments and ultimately the Act was revoked in 1948. The administrators thought that the training which they received from the settlement made them better citizens. The development of an environment required time and new recruits to the settlement were, according to the administrators, 'rude fellows of baser sort'.

However, in spite of all efforts to give the settlers every opportunity to earn good wages, it was a difficult task for anybody to train them to be industrious or hand working. With regard to the incorrigibles, Rev. Bawden wanted a separate settlement, subject to certain conditions, *viz.:* (1) incorrigibles must not be allowed to escape; (2) when a man absconded from Kavali, Bitragunta or Allur settlements for the second and third time, his family should be sent to the penal settlement; and (3) no community food should be allowed. Each should eat in proportion to his earnings. In Rev. Bawden's opinion, a true Christian, who had sympathy for the criminal tribes, should be made the Manager of the settlement. He believed that the Government officials are not the right type of persons to be put in-charge of penal settlement.

Some of these sub-divisions are exogamous, but in their common pursuit of criminal activity (robbery or snatching away or theft), they are all identical with no distinction among them. Such were the people who were brought to the settlements and dubbed as a criminal tribe. As Vennelacunti Raghavaiah puts it, (1943:5): Several aboriginal and other people of this country had been declared arbitrarily and unjustly by the British rulers as criminal tribes as early as 1871 and kept under severe restrictions.

REFERENCES

Adan, T.N., 1952, *Problem of Education and Dialects, A Paper Presented in a Conference on Scheduled Tribes and Scheduled Caste Areas,* New Delhi.

Agarwal, R.S., 1977, *Prevention of Crime,* Radiant Publishers.

Agustus Someville, 1933, *Mysterious Crime,* Calcutta.

Aiyappan, A., 1948, *Report on the Socio-economic Conditions of the Aboriginal Tribes of the Province of Madras.*

Apte, J.S., 1960, Talwada Ashram School—An Experiment in Tribal Education, *Vanyajati*, Vol. VIII, No. 2.

Bailey, G., 1960, Tribe, Caste and Nation. *Tribe and Caste in India, Contributions to Indian Sociology,* The Hague, 1961.

Baldev Raj Nayar, 1975, *Violence and Crime in India.*

Barnes and Teeters, 1951, *New Horizons in Criminology,* Prentice Hall, U.S.A.

Bateille Andre, 1977, *The Definition of a Tribe, Caste and Religion.* Ed.Romesh Thapar, Meerut.

Bearce, G.D., 1967, *British Attitudes Towards India* (1784-1858), London.

Bhadari, J.S., 1980, *The Tribal World and Its Transformation,* Bhupendra Singh and J.S.Bhadari, New Delhi.

Bhargava, B.S., 1949, *The Criminal Tribes of India, Lucknow.*

Bhattacharya, Subhas, 1977, *Social Banditry in the Bengal Presidency*, 17-65-1813, Marxist Miscellany, No.10, New Delhi.

Bhowmick, P.K., 1957, The Lodhas and Their Folk song, *Vanyajati*, Delhi.

Bhowmick, K.L., 1971, *Tribal India*, Calcutta.

Biswas, P.C., 1960, *The Ex-Criminal Tribes of Delhi State* (assisted by Indera P. Singh), Delhi.

Bodding, Rev.P.O., 1940, *Memories of Theroyal Asiattic Society of West Bengal,* Vol. 3, Calcutta.

Booth Tucker, Frederick, 1964, *Jean Gold Servant of India,* London.

Bose, Ambicacharn, 1960, *A Hand Book of Criminology*, Calcutta.

Bose, N.K., 1971, *Tribal Life in India*, New Delhi.

Bovet, L., 1951, *Psychiatric Aspects of Juvenile Delinquency,* W.H.O.,Geneva.

Chakrobarti S.S., 1964, *Crimes That Hit the Headlines,* Calcutta.

Chalavadi Satyanarayana, 1959-60, Yerukalas: An Ex-criminal Tribe of Andhra and Its Settlement (Stuartpuram), *Unpublished M.A Dissertation,* Sagar University.

Chang, Dae, H., 1976, *Criminology – A Cross-Cultural Perspective,* New Delhi.

Chaturvedi N.D, *Face to Face with Criminals,* Delhi.

Clarance, H. Partick, *The Criminal Tribes of India with Special Emphasis on the Mang Garudi.*

Crooke, W., 1896, *The Tribes and Castes of North West Provinces and Oudh,* Calcutta.

Dash Sharma, 1980, The *Passing Scene in Chotanagpur*, Ranchi.

David Arnold, 1979, Dacoity and Rural Crime in Madras', 1860-1940, *Journal of Peasant Societies.*

Dave, P.C., 1955, An Outline of the Welfare Schemes Suited for the Ex-Criminal Tribes, *Vanyajati*, Vol.III, January, No.1.

Desai, A.R., 1977, Tribe, Caste and Religion, Romesh Thapar, in *Tribes in Transition, Macmillan Camp., L of India.*

Dube, S.K. and Madhur, F., 1967, *A Study of the Tribal People Areas of M.P., Published by Tribal Research and Development Institute, Bhopal.*

Dubey, S.M. and Tarna Murdia, 1976, *Administration of Policy and Programmes for Backward Classes in India,* New Delhi.

Edwards C.M, 1931, Criminal Tribes at Hubli, West Minister.

Edwards, S.M., 1924, Crime in India, London.

Edwards, S.M. and Carett, H.L.O., 1976, Mughal Rule in India, Delhi.

Elwin, Verrier, 1947, The Muria and Their Chotul, Bombay.

Eysenck, H.J., 1971, Crime and Personality, London.

Fisher, R.J. and Austria, 1981, Nomadic Groups in the Caste System in India, Vol. 61, No.1, March.

Ghosh, 1969, Law Breakers and Keepers of Peace, Calcutta.

Ghurye, G.S., 1969, The Aboriginals: So Called and Their Future, Bombay.

Gillen, 1945, Criminology and Penology, New York.

Gupta, M.K.D., 1963, the Problem of Tribal Education and the Santhals, New Delhi.

Gupta, Rishi Ram and Matur, J.S., Social Pathology of Denotified Tribes.

Gupta, R.K., 1980, Implementation of Tribal Welfare Projects (Bidisa – A Case Study), Man and Life, Journal of the Institute of Social Research and applied Anthropology, Calcutta.

Haimendorf, Christopher, von Fureer, 1943, The Aboriginal Tribes, Hyderabad, Vol.I, The Chenchus, London.

Haral, G.P., 1968, Denotified Community and Their Problems of Rehabilitation, *The Indian Journal of Social Work*, Vol. XXVIII.

Hutton, J, H., 1973, Caste in India—Its Nature, Function and Origin (first published in 1946), Bombay.

Jaspal Singh, 1976, Reformation of Ex-Criminal Tribes.

Jaya Singh Visuvathas, (n.d.), Social and Economic Aspects of Theft, *Indian Journal of Criminology.*

Jawaharlal Nehru, *Publications Division*, Government of India, 1955.

Joseph, A., 1967, Yerukala Traditional Justice, *Tribal World,* Vol.4, Hyderabad.

Kamaladevi Chattopadhyaya, 1978, *Tribalism in India,* New Delhi.

Kapadia, K.M., 1952, The Criminal Tribes of India, *Sociological Bulletin.*

Kelkar, Ashok, R., 1972, Language Study in the Integration of Tribal Population in India, *Vivekananda Kendra Patrika.*

Lalitha, V., 1977, Socio-economic and Administrative Aspects of an ex-Criminal Tribe (*unpublished M.Phil, Thesis*).

—1978, Historical Background of Kapparallatippa Settlement, *Proceedings of A.P History Congress.*

—1981, Denotified Communities of Andhra Pradesh—Some Problems of Rehabilitation, *Proceedings of A.P History Congress.*

—1982, Ethnographic Background of Yerukalas, *Proceedings of A.P History Congress.*

Lavanam and Hemalatha Lavanam, 1975, The Problem of Denotified Tribes—An Experiment of Stuartpuram.

Laxmanna Mamata, 1982, *Roots of Delinquency, Social Welfare,* Vol. XXIX.

Lewis John, Gillean, 1931, *Taming a Criminal,* London.

Luiz, A.A.D., 1962, Tribes of Kerala, New Delhi.

Maity, S., Emerging Problems of the Ex-Criminal Tribe: Lodhas of West Bengal, Seminar on Integrated Tribal Development Plans: Preparation and Implementation at National Institute of Community Development, Hyderabad.

Majumdar, D.N and Madan, T.N., 1956, An Introduction to Social Anthropology, New Delhi.

Mehta B.H., Ex-Criminal Groups in *India, Indian Journal of Social Work*, 1955-56.

Mehta B.H., (n.d.), Tribal Development Since Independence, *Tribal Souvenir.*

Merton, R.K., 1967, Social Theory and Social Structure, New Delhi.

Mithilesh Gupta, 1964, Rehabilitation of Criminal Tribes, *The Eastern Anthropologist,* Vol.XVII, No.1, Jan-April.

Mukherjee, S.K., 1974, Crime Statistics in India, A Commentary, *Indian Journal of Criminology,* Vol.II, No.2.

Mullaly, 1912, *The Criminal Classes of Madras Presidency,* Madras.

Nihar Ranjan Ray, 1922, *Tribal Situation in India, An Introductory Address in a Seminar,* ed, K.Suresh Singh, Simla.

Panakal, J.J., 1973, *An Agenda for Criminology, Indian Journal of Criminology, Madras.*

Papa Rao Naidu M, 1905, *History of Railway Thieves, Madras.*

—1905, *Criminal Tribes of India, The History of Korawaras,* Yerukulas or Kaikaries, Madras.

Parthasaradhi, Jakka., 1988, *The Yerukala Ethnographic Study*, Calcutta.

Paul Chowdary, D., 1966, *A Hand Book on Social Welfare (Institute of Social Sciences, Agra University),* Delhi.

Raghavaiah, V., 1943, The Problem of Criminal Tribes, Nellore—quoted from Mr.Stephen's Statement Made in 1872 (the member for law and order).

Ramachandra Sastry, 1916, *Neramulu Cheyu Jatula Charitramulu* (Telugu), Vijayawada.

Rangaiah Desabhatla, 1950, *Yerukulas, Tribes of India*, Delhi.

Ray, P.P.C., 1980, *The Tribal World and Its Transformation*, ed. Bhupinder Singh and J.S Bhandari, New Delhi.

Roy Burman, B.K., 1972, Integrated Area Approach to the Problems of the Hill Tribes of North-East India, Tribal Situation in India *(Proceedings of a Seminar, Indian Institute of Advanced Study, Simla).*

Sayena, N.S., 1975, Main Reasons for Increase in Crime in India in Recent Years, *The Indian Journal of Public Administration.*

Sikka, K.D., 1981, After-care Programme for Juveniles. Where Does it Stand Today? The Indian Journal of Social Work, Tata Institute of Social Work, Bombay (*unpublished M.Phil. Thesis*).

Simhadir, Y.S., 1976, Changing Criminal Behaviour of an Ex-criminal Tribe in an *Indian Village, Indian Journal of Criminology.*

Singh, M.K., (n.d.), Women and Crime Phenomenon, *Indian Journal of Social Work.*

Srivastava, R.S., 1974, Crime and Society, *Indian Journal of Criminology, Madras.*

Srinivasa Raghava Iyenger, 1983, *Memorandum of the Progress of Madras Presidency During the Last Forty Years of British Administration.*

Surajit Sinha, 1981, *Tribes and Indian Civilisation, Transformation Process in Modern India,* Man In India.

Shashi.S.S. 1995, *Tribes of Andhra Pradesh.* Anmoul Publications Pvt Ltd New Delhi.

Subba Ramaraju, Sudhakar, C. *Developmental Programmes and Social Transfermation.* Associated Publishers, New Delhi-2006.

Thurston, Edgar, 1909, *Castes and Tribes of Southern India,* Vol.III, Madras.

Tribal Welfare Department, 1987, *Tribal Welfare Activities in Andhra Pradesh.*

Tribes of A.P., *Tribal Culture Research and Training Institute,* 2001, *Hyderabad.*

Troisi Jesh, 1979, *Social Movements Among the Santhals, Social Movements in India* Vol.II, ed., M.S.A., Rao, New Delhi.

Umamohan, C. A.Naganna, Occupational Changes and Mobility: An Intra-Generational Study of Yerukulas in Rayalaseema Region of AP. National *Seminar on 3rd and 4th November, 2006.* Dravidian University, Kuppam.

Umamohan, C, Naganna, A., "Yerukula Tribes and Social Transformation," Bharatiya Adimajathi Sevak Sangh (Vanyagati), New Delhi 2006.

Umamohan, C. A.Naganna, Globalisation: Continuity and Change of Livelihood and Interdependence: A Study of Yerukula Tribe (*paper submitted at the National Seminar on Globalisation*: Indian Society, Continuities and Change Hyderabad, 7th April, 2006).

Vanikar, P.G., (n.d.), Missionary Approach to Tribal Welfare, *Tribal Souvenir.*

Venkata Rao, S., 1962, *A Century of Tribal Politics,* New Delhi.

Venugopal Rao, S., 1962, *Facets of Crime.*

Vidyathi, L.P., 1964, *Culture Contours of Tribal Bihar,* Calcutta.

The Setting

SECTION I

Andhra Pradesh Profile With Reference To Tribals

Andhra Pradesh is contiguous to Tamil Nadu in the South, Karnataka in the South-West, Maharastra in the West-North, Madhya Pradesh in the North and Orissa in the North-East. Out of the total geographical area of the State, 23 per cent (64,154 sq. kms) comes under forests. Thus the 33 tribes who are living in the forests of Andhra Pradesh are scattered over the entire area of the State. The scheduled areas of the State touch the borders of neighbouring States of Orissa, Madhya Pradesh and Maharashtra. The forest area has hill ranges and chequered valleys traversed by hill streams of the Eastern Ghats and the forests flanking the mighty Godavari and Krishna rivers constitute the traditional habitats of the tribes. Each tribe has fashioned its arti-facts, mentis-facts and socio-facts in accordance with its environment and genius (Pratap, D.R.1975).

Andhra Pradesh is one of the States with a large chunk of population of Scheduled Tribes. Scheduled Tribe population in the State stood at 76.210 lakhs as per the 2001 Census, the constituting 6.59 per cent of the total population of the State (GO1, 2001). The extent of the Scheduled Areas in the State is 31,485.34 sq. kms., which constitutes about 11 per cent of the total area of the State. The Scheduled Areas fall in the nine districts of Srikakulam, Vizianagaram, Visakhapatnam, West Godavari, East Godavari, Khammam, Warangal, Mahaboobnagar and Adilabad. Of the total population, 26.05 lakh tribals accounting for 62.03 per cent live in the Scheduled Areas while rummage 15.94 lakhs accounting for 37.97 per cent reside in the non-Scheduled Areas where they are interspersed with the advanced population (Govt. of A.P, 1993). Most of the Scheduled Areas in the State are covered with dense forests which are endowed with rich mineral and forest wealth. The difficult and inaccessible terrain rendered tribal societies closed ones with distinctive socio-cultural patterns of their own. Their physical and social isolation coupled with low standards of living marks them off from the rest of population.

The tribal situation in Andhra Pradesh presents a complex and uneven picture with considerable social diversity. The tribals living in the State are broadly divided into 33 ethnic groups. There is considerable variation in the size, mode of living and levels of development among these tribal groups apart from differences in language and dialect. On the basis of geo-ethnic characteristics, the tribal areas of Andhra Pradesh can be divided into the following five geographical regions:

1. *Gond-Kolam Region*—the tribal areas of Adilabad district;
2. *Koya-Konda Reddi Region*—Tribal areas of Karimnagar, Warangal, Khammam, West Godavari and East Godavari districts along Godavari gorages;
3. *Ghond-Savara Region*—Tribal areas of Visakhapatnam, Vizanagarm, and Srikakulam districts;
4. *Chenchu Region*—Tribal Areas of Mahaboobnagar, Nalgonda, Kurnool, Prakasam and Guntur districts;
5. *Plain Areas*—Areas of habitation of Yanadis, Yerukulas and Banjaras of Lambadas or Sugalis (GO1, 1989).

The distribution of Scheduled Tribe population among the different district of Andhra Pradesh is presented in Table 3.1. It is clear from the table that the percentage share of Scheduled Tribe population in the total population is the

Table 3.1. District-wise Population of Scheduled Tribes of Andhra Pradesh-2001 Census

Sl. No.	Name of the District	Total Population (In Lakhs)	ST Population (In Lakhs)	% ST Population to Total Population
1	Adilabad	24.88	4.16	16.74
2	Nizamabad	23.45	1.65	7.07
3	Karimnagar	34.91	0.91	2.60
4	Medak	26.70	1.34	5.04
5	Hyderabad	38.29	0.34	0.90
6	Rangareddi	35.75	1.46	4.09
7	Mahabubnagar	35.13	2.78	7.93
8	Nalgonda	32.47	3.42	10.55
9	Warangal	32.46	4.57	14.10
10	Khammam	25.78	6.82	26.47
11	Kadapa	26.01	0.61	2.36
12	Kurnool	35.29	0.70	1.97
13	Anantapur	36.40	1.27	3.49
14	Chittoor	37.45	1.28	3.42
15	Srikakulam	25.37	1.52	5.96
16	Vizianagaram	22.49	2.14	9.55
17	Visakapatnam	38.32	5.57	14.55
18	East Godavari	49.01	1.91	3.91
19	West Godavari	38.03	0.97	2.54
20	Krishna	41.87	1.07	2.57
21	Guntur	44.65	2.08	4.66
22	Prakasam	30.59	1.18	3.86
23	Nellore	26.68	2.42	9.08

Source: Census of India, 2001

highest in Khammam district followed by Adilabad, Visakhapatnam, Warangal, Nalgonda, Vijayanagram, Nellore and Mahaboobnagar.

The total population of Andhra Pradesh, as per the 2001 Census, is 76,210,007. Of which, 5,024,104 (6.6 per cent) are Scheduled Tribes (STs). The ST population constitutes 6 per cent of the country's ST population. The Scheduled Castes and Scheduled Tribes Orders (Amendment) Act, 1976 have notified 33 STs in the state. Out of the 33 STs, five namely, *Goudu, Malis, Nayaks, Thoti* and *Valmiki* have been notified with an area restriction. Goudu, Nayaks and Valmiki have been notified in the Agency tracts area, which comprises Srikakulum, Vizianagaram, Visakhapatnam, East Godavari, West Godavari and Khammam districts. Malis have been notified in the state excluding Adilabad, Hyderabad, Karimnagar, Khammam, Mahbubnagar, Medak, Nalgonda, Nizamabad and Warangal districts. Thoti have been notified in the Adilabad, Hyderabad, Karimnagar, Khammam, Mahbubnagar, Medak, Nalgonda, Nizamabad and Warangal districts.

Twelve tribes namely: *Bodo Gadaba, Gutob Gadaba, Bondo Poraja, Khond Poroja, Parangiperja, Chenchu, Dongaria Khonds, Kuttiya Kondhs, Kolam, Kondareddis, Konda Savaras,* and *Thoti* have been recognised as Primitive Tribal Groups (PTGs). Except Kondareddis and Thoti, population on other PTGs are not available separately as these are notified as sub-groups/sections of main communities. The population of Kondareddis and Thoti is 83,096 and 2,074 respectively, as per the 2001 Census.

The growth rate of ST population in the decade 1991-2001 at 19.6 per cent has been higher if compared to the overall growth rate of 14.6 per cent of the state population as a whole. Among the numerically major STs, highest growth rate of 36 per cent has been recorded in the case of Sugalis, followed by Koya (24.4 per cent), Gond (18.9 per cent), Yenadis (16.8 per cent) and Yerukulas (12.8 per cent).

Population—Size and Distribution

Out of the 33 STs, *Sugalis* are numerically the largest ST with a population of 2,077,947 constituting 41.4 per cent of the state's ST population. They are followed by *Koya* 568,019 (11.3 per cent), *Yenadis* 462,167 (9.2 per cent), *Yerukulas* 437,459 (8.7 per cent) and *Gond* 252,038 (5 per cent). These five STs together account for 76 per cent of the ST population of the state.

Of the total ST population, 92.5 per cent are residing in rural areas. Among the major STs, Gond have the highest (97.6 per cent) rural population, followed by Koya (95.5 per cent), Sugalis (93.7 per cent), Yenadis (86.4 per cent) and Yerukulas (77.5 per cent). District-wise distribution of ST population shows that they are mainly concentrated in the districts of Khammam, Visakhapatnam, Warangal, Adilabad and Nalgonda. These five districts constitute 48.9 per cent of the total ST population of the state.

Literacy and Educational Level

Literacy and level of education are two basic indicators of the level of development achieved by a group/society. The literacy results in a more awareness besides contributing to the overall improvement of health, hygiene and other social conditions. According to 2001 Census, percentage of literate persons (those who can read and write with understanding), aged 7 years and above, among ST population of Andhra Pradesh is 37 per cent, which is lower than 60.5 per cent reported for state population as a whole. The literacy data show that the ST population of the state has made significant improvement in literacy during the decade 1991-2001. The literacy rate, which was 17.1 per cent in 1991, has increased by 19.9 percentage points in 2001. But in comparison to other states/UTs, the position of ST population of Andhra Pradesh is not satisfactory. It is just above Uttar Pradesh (35.1 per cent) and Bihar (28.2 per cent), which are bottom two states in literacy rate for ST population among all states/UTs. At the district level, the highest literacy rate has been recorded in Hyderabad (55.4 per cent) and the lowest in Mahbubnagar (25.8 per cent)

Table 3.2. Educational Levels Attained by Major Scheduled Tribes

Name of the Tribe	Litera-ture with out edu-cational levels	Below prim-ary	Prim-ary	Middle	Metric/ Secon-dary High Seco-ndary/ Interme-diate. etc.	Tech-nical & Non-Tech-nical	Gradu-ate & above
All STs	6.3	42.0	28.4	8.5	12.3	0.6	1.8
Sugali	5.6	43.6	25.7	8.7	13.3	0.8	2.3
Koya	6.5	43.4	29.2	8.5	10.9	0.4	1.2
Gond	7.7	50.0	25.1	7.2	9.1	0.2	0.6
Yanadi	9.7	47.0	29.7	5.3	6.9	0.4	1.1
Yerukula	4.4	32.2	30.8	10.3	17.7	1.3	3.3

Source: Office of the Registrar General, India, 2001.

Among the major STs, Yerukulas have reported the highest literacy rate (45.4 per cent), followed by Koya (41.8 per cent), Gond (36.4 per cent), Yenadis (35.3 per cent) and Sugalis (34.3 per cent). The female literacy rate of 26.1 per cent among the ST population is matter of concern as almost a fourth of ST females are illiterate in the state.

Out of total literates, 48.3 per cent are literates without any educational level or have attained below Primary level. The literates, who have attained education up to Primary level and Middle level, constitute 28.4 per cent and 8.5 per cent respectively. 12.3 per cent are having educational level up to Matric/Higher Secondary etc. levels, implying that every 8th ST literate is a Matriculate. Literates with educational level of Graduation and above are 1.8 per cent. Individually, Yerukulas (3.3 per cent) have the highest percentage of Graduate and above educational level.

The educational level table also shows that the drop out is conspicuous after the Primary level and again after Matric/

Secondary levels. This pattern is consistent among all the major SCs.

Population in the age group 5-14 years are the potential students. Only 60.7 per cent of the ST population in this age group has been attending various educational institutions.

Each tribe has its own distinct social and economic organisation and each tribe speaks its own dialect. Because of several development measures and contact with non-tribals, the tribal their cultures currently are undergoing transformation. As a result some tribes no longer possess all of the typical characteristics of a tribe.

Kurnool District Profile with Reference To Tribals

The present study is carried out in two district of Rayalaseema, namely Anantapur and Kurnool districts of Rayalaseema region of Andhra Pradesh.

Kurnool district was the erstwhile capital of the former Nawabs and at present the headquarters of the District. The name "Kurnool" is said to have been derived from *'Kandenvolu'*. According to the tradition in the 11 century A.D, the Vadders who carved stones for the construction of temple at Alampur used the site on which the town now stands as a halting place before crossing the river Thungabhadra and greased their cart wheel with oil locally supplied by some of the oil mongers and called the place "Kandenavolu" which subsequently come to be known as Kurnool, the town of 'Kandena' or grease.

Kurnool District is one of the four districts of Rayalaseema region of Andhra Pradesh State. Kurnool was the capital of Andhra Pradesh from 1st October 1953 to 31st October, 1956. It is also regarded as "Gateway of Rayalaseema".

Location and Composition: Kurnool district lies between the Northern latitude of 14.54 and 16.11 eastern latitudes of 76.58 and 78.25. The district is bounded on the North by Thungabhadra and Krishna rivers as well as Mahaboobnagar district, on the South by Kadapa and Anantapur districts, on the West by Karnataka State and East by Prakasam District. The area of the District is 17,648 sq.kms. Covered by 29,73,024 population as per 1991 Census with a density of 168 persons per sq.km.

At present Kurnool District comprise 3 revenue divisions, (Kurnool, Nandyal and Adoni), 54 Revenue Mandals, 53 Mandal Parishads, 821 Gram Panchayats and 918 Revenue villages.

Physiography: Nallamals and Erramals are the two important mountain ranges the District, running parallel from North to South. The Erramalas divide the District into two well defined tracks from East and West. Between Erramals and Nallamlas lies the eastern part of the District comprising 25 mandals. This tract is crossed by the crest of Krishna and Pennar, watershed at the Northern part of Pagidyala mandal at about 1000 ft. above the sea level. Major part of its tract is predominantly black cotton soil.

The Western tract comprises 28 mandals and the terrain here slopes from South to North and it is drained by the river Hundri which joins the river Thungabhadra at Kurnool. The soil in the North-Western traversed parts by the river Hundri are black cotton while the South-Eastern parts are predominantly poor red soil.

Climate: the climate of the District is normal. In the months of January, February and March the climate is usually pleasant with moderate winds from South-West. April and May are hottest months of the year, when the wind shifts to South-West with increased force and brings welcome showers by the end of May. During the succeeding four months the wind blows from Western side in major parts of the district and brings fair quantum of rainfall. By the end of September the wind is light and pleasant forecasting the onset of North-East Monsoons. In November and December the weather is fine. Rainfall is rare and the wind is light with occurrence of heavy dew. District normal rainfall is 630 mm.

Rivers: the principal rivers flowing in the district are the Thungabhadra and Hundri, its tributary, Krishna and Kunderu.

Flora, Forest and Fauna: The total area under forests is 7,86,412 acres accounting for about 18 per cent of the total geographical area of the district. The major parts of the forest area confine mainly to the Nallamalas including its extensions, the Erramalas and a part of the Velikonds. The forest covering the Erramalas and Velikondas with inferior type bamboo with timber species occurs fairly over extensive areas in the district. Tamarind and Beedi leaves are the important minor forcst produce of the district.

Rainfall: All mandals in Kurnool District get rain from South-West and North-East Monsoons. The average rainfall in the year 1990-91 was 629.2 mm and in 1995-96 it was 60.50 mm. the average rainfall of the district was 630 mm.

Population: Kurnool District with a population of 3,529,494 as per 2001 Census occupies 11th place among the districts of Andhra Pradesh and third place in the population of Rayalaseema region. Kurnool District accounts for 4.47 per cent of the total population of Andhra Pradesh (6,63,545,539) and 25.47 per cent of the population of Rayalaseema region of the State (1,16,68,044). Kurnool District is one of the sparsely population district in Andhra Pradesh with a density of 168 persons per sq.km. As against the State coverage of 173 per sq.km. The sex ratio in Kurnool district was 965 females for every 1000 males. Of the total population urban population constitutes 25.85 per cent in the district as against 26.84 per cent for the State as a whole. The population of the scheduled castes in Kurnool district accounts for 17.81 per cent of the total population of the district (15.92 per cent in Andhra Pradesh) and the population of the scheduled tribes constitute. 1.97 per cent of the total population of the district (6.31 per cent in Andhra Pradesh).

Table 3.3. Population Characteristics of Kurnool District

Sl. No.	Item	Unit	
1	Population	Lakhs	35.29
	Males	Lakhs	17.96
	Females	Lakhs	17.33
2	Rural Population	Lakhs	27.12
3	Urban Population	Lakhs	8.17
4	Urban Population as % to Total	%	23.2
5	Population of Scheduled Castes	%	17.08
6	Population of Scheduled Tribes	%	2.0
7	Population (0-6)		537606
8	Sex-ratio	No	965
9	Sex-ratio (0-6)	No	958
10	Sex-ratio S.C.	No	961
11	Sex-ratio S.T.	No	929
12	No. of Households	No	699191
13	Household size	No	5.0
14	Literacy Rate		53.2
	Males		66.0
	Females		40.0
15	Revenue Divisions	No	3
16	Revenue Mandals	No	54
17	Total Number of Villages	No	2631

Source: 1. Hand Book of Kurnool District Statistics, Kurnool, 2002-03.
2. Census of India, 2001.

Literacy Levels: The percentage of literates in the total population of Kurnool District as per 1991 Census is 33 per cent as against 44.09 per cent for the State and rural urban break up of literacy rates in the district indicates that 37.99 per cent of rural population and 58.64 per cent of urban population are literates respectively.

There are about 11 towns in the district with total population of 29,73,709 as per 1991 census. About 44.25 per cent of the tribal populations are main workers and 32.3 per cent are agricultural workers as per 1991 census. In the district there are 15.62 per cent and 1.95 per cent belongs to scheduled castes and scheduled tribes respectively. There are 6,91,574 literates and accounts for 28.73 per cent of the total population. Out of this, about 4, 90,246 (39.96 per cent) are male and 2,01,328 (17.06 per cent) are female as per 1991 census. There are about 2161 primary schools, 603 upper primary high schools, 460 High Schools, 61 Junior Colleges, 30 Degree Colleges, one Medical Collage 5 Engineering Colleges, 3 Polytechnic Colleges and 7 Industrial Training Institutions of the district during 1995-2002 rendering educational facilities to the people living in the district. There are about 27 hospitals, 15 dispensaries and 70 Public Health Centres of the district during 1995-2002 rendering Medical Services to the people living in the district.

Education: There are as many as 2,328 educational institutions apart from intermediate, degree, P.G.Centres, medical, engineering colleges in the district. The district as also several private educational institutions. However, majority of these institutions are located in urban and semi-urban areas.

Hospitals: The District has one popular general hospital at the headquarters. There are in all 19 hospitals, 89 dispensaries and one hospital for special treatment for eye, 418 government doctors and the total bed strength is 1,632. There are two Ayurvedic hospitals and eight Ayurvedic dispensaries with eight doctors are situated in the District. There is one Unani hospital and six dispensaries with eight doctors and three Homoeo hospitals with three doctors in Kurnool District.

Occupational Distribution: The agricultural workers (cultivators plus agricultural labours) constitute a very high proportion to the total working population. Cultivators and agricultural labours together formed 72.04 per cent of the total work force in the district as against 64.76 per cent for the State as whole. Thus a major portion of the work force is engaged in the agricultural sector.

Table 3.4. Work Participation of Kurnool District

Sl. No.	Item	Unit	Persons	Male	Female
1.	Total Workers	No	1745220	1011044	734176
2.	Proportion of Non-workers	%	50.6	43.7	57.6
4.	Main Workers	%	42.5	51.4	33.3
5.	Marginal workers	%	6.9	4.9	9.1
	Proportion to total workers				
	Cultivators	%	22.2	24.8	18.5
6.	Agricultural Labour	%	46.0	34.2	62.3
	Household Industry	%	3.5	2.8	4.5
	Other Workers	%	26.7	35.3	13.6
7.	Work Participation Rate	%	28.3	38.2	14.7

Source: 1. Hand Book of Kurnool District Statistics, Kurnool, 2002-03.
2. Census of India, 2001.

Land Utilisation: Agriculture is the main occupation of the people of Kurnool District. About seventy two per cent of the working population is engaged in agricultural sector. The pattern of the land utilisation in the district is that 51.55 per cent of the total geographical area is under forest batten lands, cultivable waste, grounding lands etc., put together constitute the uncultivated area.

Source of irrigation: In Kurnool District 3 major irrigational, 1 medium irrigational and 609 small irrigational project are the major sources of irrigation. If the irrigational facilities available in Kurnool District are measured it is evident that only 16.72 per cent of net sown area was irrigated from all sources during the year 1993-94 as against 37.55 per cent for the State as a whole. The important sources of irrigation in the district are canals, tanks and wells. The canals worth mentioning are K.C.Canal, Thungabhadra project Low Level and High Level Canal, Zureru Project, and Gajuladinne Project. The total irrigated area is about 3,74,981 acres. Canals are the principal sources of irrigation covering 46.95 per cent of the total net irrigated area in the district. Wells are the next important source of irrigation covering 25.19 per cent to the total net irrigated area. The area irrigated by tanks is 16.53 per cent. The area irrigated by other sources is lowest in the district *i.e.,* 11.33 per cent to the total net irrigated area.

Transport and Communication: The district has sufficient transport facilities. The most important railway line in the district is North-West main line of the Southern Railways connecting Chennai in the South and Mumbai in the West. All important towns and villages in the District are well connected by a network of roads. On an average, 90 per cent of the villages have been connected by roads and remaining villages by kutcha roads.

Important Trading Centres: All the erstwhile taluk headquarters in Kurnool District are important wholesale trading centres Kurnool, Adoni, Nandyal and Yemmiganur have a prime place among them. These trading centres are also offering seasonal as well as full employment to the rural labour. Further, there are many weekly markets functioning in the District. In fact these are the places where the rural labour can purchase all the consumer goods.

Industrial Profile: The Rayalaseema region of Kurnool District has nearly 900 industrial units, medium and small. These units are mostly agro-based and provide employment to nearly 25,000 workers. Kurnool district possesses enormous deposits of limestone suitable for cement production and as a result of which cement industry is prospering in the District. The labourers belonging to these places are also gainfully employed. Further, handloom weaving is also an important cottage industry in the district.

ANANTAPUR DISTRICT PROFILE WITH REFERENCE TO TRIBALS

Historical Background

Anantapur District was formed in the year 1882 having been separated from Bellary district. Later on, it was expanded with the addition of Revenue Mandals of Kadiri, Mudigubba, Nallamada, N.P.Kunta, Talupula, Nallacheruvu, O.D.Cheruvu, Tanakal, Amadagur and Gandlapenta (previous Kadiri Taluk) from Cuddapah District in the year 1910. During the year 1956, the present Revenue Mandals of Rayadurg, D.Hirehal, Kanekal, Bommanahal and Gummagatta of Bellary District were added to Anantapur District. The District has been divided into 3 Revenue Divisions consisting of 63 Revenue Mandals (Anantapur Division 20, Dharmavaram Division 17 and Penukonda Division 26).

Boundaries and Topography

Anantapur District lies between 13'-40' and 15'-15' Northern Latitude and 76'-50' and 78'-30' Eastern Longitude. It is bounded by Bellary, Kurnool District on the North, Kadapa and Kolar District of Karnataka on South East and North respectively. The District is roughly oblong in shape, the longer side running north to South with a portion of Chitradurg District of Karnataka State intruding into it from west between Kundurpi and Amarapuram Mandals.

The District may be divided into 3 Natural Divisions. They are: 1) Northern Mandal of Rayadurg, Kanekal, Beluguppa Gooty, Guntakal, Vajrakarur, Uravakonda, Vidapanakal, Yadiki, Tadipatri, Putlur and Yellanur containing larger areas of Black Cotton soils; (2) Kalyandurg, Kambadur, Settur, Brahmasamudram, Ramagiri, Kanaganapalli, C.K.Palli, Dharmavaram, Bathalapalli, Tadimarri, Mudigubba, Anantapur, Kudair, Pamidi and Peddavadugur in the center which are mainly made up of arid Treeless, expense of poor Red Soils; (3) High Level Land of Penukonda, Roddam, Somandepalli, Hindupur, Lepakshi, Chilamathur, Madakasira, Rolla, Gudibanda and Agali which connects with Mysore plateau at higher elevation of the rest of the District. This part has average sandy red soils of normal productivity.

Forests

The Forests in the District are thin and scanty. The Muchukota Hills about 35 kms. in length run from North of Gooty Town upto extreme Southern Corner of Tadipatri and Yadiki Mandals. Another line of Hills starts from West of Gooty Mandal and run 80 kms. called by name Nagasamudram Hills. The Mallappakonda Range begins at Dharmavaram and runs into Karnataka State.

The Penukonda Range which starts in the South of Dharmavaram through Penukonda and Hindupur proceeds to Karnataka State.

In Madakasira, the hills divide Rolla and Agali Mandals into Southern and Northern portions.

Rivers

The important river in the District is Pennar. It has its origin in the Nandi Hills of Karnataka State where it is called

'Uttarapinakini' and enters this District in the extreme South of Hindupur Mandal and flows through Parigi, Roddam, Ramagiri, Kambadur, Kalyandurg, Beluguppa, Uravakonda, Vajrakarur, Pamidi, Peddavadugur, Peddapappur and Tadipatri Mandals and finally enters Cuddapah District.

There is one Major Irrigation Project T.B.P.H.L.C., and 3 Medium Irrigation Projects. 1. Upper Pennar Project, 2.Bhairavanithippa Project, 3.Chennarayaswamy Gudi.

The Geographical position of the Peninsula render it, the driest part of the State and hence, Agriculture conditions are more often precarious. Monsoons also evades this part due to its unfortunate location. Being far from the East coast, it does not enjoy the full benefits of North East Monsoons and being cut off by the high western Ghats, the South West Monsoon are also prevented from penetrating and punching the thirst of these parched soils. It is therefore seen; the district is deprived of both the monsoons and subjected to droughts due to bad seasons. The normal rainfall of the district is 552.0 MMs. by which it secures least rainfall when compared to Rayalaseema and other parts of Andhra Pradesh. The normal rainfall for the South West Monsoon period is 338.0 MMs. which forms about 61.2 per cent of the total rainfall for the year. The failure of the rains in this South-West monsoon period of June to September will lead the District to drought by failure of crops. The rainfall for North East monsoon period is 156.0 MMs. only, which forms 28.3 per cent MMs. of the total rainfall for the year (October to December). The other months are almost dry March, April and May are warm months when the normal daily maximum temperature ranges between 29.1 C November, December and January are cooler months when the temperature falls about 17.2 C, Hindupur, Parigi,

Lepakshi, Chilamathur, Agali, Rolla and Madakasira Mandals being at High Elevation are more cooler than the rest of the Mandals in the District.

Soils

The soils in Anantapur District are predominantly red except Kanekal, Bommanahal, Vidapanakal, Uravakonda, Vajrakarur, Guntakal, Gooty, Pamidi, Peddavadugur, Yadiki, Tadipatri, Yellanur, Peddapappur and Putlur. In these Mandals occur with red and black soils occur almost in equal proportion. Thus 76 per cent red soils, 24 per cent are black soil.

Population Distribution of Anantapur In 1971 to 2001

There are 940 inhabited villages, out of 964 total Revenue villages of the District. The number of villages in size group of 500 to 1999 forms 36.06 per cent of the total inhabited villages. The size group of 2000 to 4999 forms 38.19 per cent and the size group of 5000 to 9999 forms 12.34 per cent only out of total villages, while 85 villages (9.04%) of total inhabited villages are having population less than 500. There are 26 villages with more than 10000 population excluding Towns.

Table 3.5

Period	Total	Rural	Urban	% of Growth Rate
1971	2115321	1739531	375790	19.7
1981	2548012	2017095	530917	20.47
1991	3180863	2432810	748053	24.93
2001	3640478	2720915	919563	14.45

• Hand book of Anantapur District Statistics, 2002-03

There are 10 Towns in Anantapur District as per 2001 Census. The following Table 3.6 gives the growth of population of towns from 1991 to 2001.

Table 3.6. The Growth of population of Towns/Municipalities in Anantapur District

Name of the Mandal	Civic & Administrative status in 2001 census	Population			% of growth
		1981	1991	2001	
Anantapur	Municipality	119531	174924	252298	25.09
Guntakal	Municipality	84599	107592	117103	8.84
Hindupur	Municipality	55091	104651	125074	19.52
Kadiri	Municipality	52774	63078	76252	20.89
Tadipatri	Municipality	53939	71068	86843	22.20
Dharmavaram	Municipality	50969	78961	103357	30.90
Rayadurg	Municipality	32745	40845	54125	32.51
Gooty	Panchayat Board	29302	37814	43389	14.74
Uravakonda	Panchayat Board	21754	27679	31856	15.09
Kalyandurg	Panchayat Board	17049	23106	29266	26.66

• Handbook of Anantapur District Statistics, 2002-03

The density of population of the District is 190 per sq. km, against (277) of the State. The population of Rural and Urban to the total population of the District workout to 75 per cent and 25 per cent in 2001 Census as against 87.5 per cent of 1991 Census. There are 958 Females per 1000 Males in 2001 Census.

The working force in the total population of District forms 48.83 per cent as per 2001 census out of which 26 per cent are in the Agriculture Sector.

Land Utilisation

The total geographical area of the district is 19.13 lakh hectares. The land utilisation pattern as available in the district during the year 2002-2003.

The cultivated area of the District is 10.44 lakh hectares. Out of which 9.00 lakh hectares is under Kharif and 1.44 lakh hectares, is under Rabi Season during the year 2002-2003.

The District occupies the lowest position in respect of irrigation facilities with only 14.98 per cent of the gross cropped area during 2002-2003.

Out of the gross irrigated area of 1.56 lakh hectares during 2002-2003, canals accounted for 13.23 per cent tanks, 1.39 per cent, tube wells 64.83 per cent wells 19.22 per cent and other sources 1.33 per cent. All the principal sources except canals are non-precarious.

Natural Resources

(a) Forests : The District is not rich in the Forest Wealth. The name 'Forest' in Anantapur District does not indicate any dense tree population with thick foliage of vermiform of pastures.

Iron ore node steatite is the minerals occurring in the district. There are however no large sized integrals occurring in the district. There are 2 Cement Factories in Tadipatri Mandal one in the Public Sector and the other in private sector. The construction work of L&T Factory is completed and started production.

Place of Tourist Importance

(a) Gugudu: The village in Narpala Mandal is at a distance of 29 kms from Anantapur and is situated among the Mutchukota Hills. It is known for its Moharum Festival and Sri Kullai Swamy is the name of the much venerated saint. Barren women are said to become fertile by paying a visit to the shrine. Fire walking ceremony is conducted on the night of the 11th day of Moharrum. There is also a Sri Anjaneya Swamy Temple near by the abode of Sri Kullai Swamy.

(b) Lepakshi: The village is situated at a distance of 14 kms from Hindupur Town in Lepakshi Mandal. This place is a famous pilgrim centre known for its Veerabhadra Temple and the huge stone 'Nandi' which stands nearby. The place is also associated with the travellers of Lord Sri Ram. The temple is veritable treasure of sculpture and architecture. Large numbers of pilgrims visit the place on 'Shivarathri' and other Saivite festival days.

(c) Kasapuram: The place is about 4 kms north of Guntakal and is known for the temple of Nettikanti Veera Anjaneya Swamy. Hindu pilgrims from several parts of Anantapur, Kurnool and Bellary districts congregate here in large number especially on Saturdays and worship the deity, besides performing marriages and tonsure ceremonies. Even Muslims of the surrounding areas visit the place and make their offerings to this deity. A huge procession is taken out once in a year on the day next to the Telugu New Year Day.

(d) Alurkona: This place is at a distance of 5 kms. from Tadpatri and is known for the Sri Ranganatha Swamy Temple built on the top of the hill by Yerramaraju, a Chieftain of Bukkarayalu in 1330.There is a waterfall nearby with perennial spring. It is not only a pilgrim centre but also a picnic spot on account of the scenic beauty of the place. Thousands of pilgrims visit the place all round the year and perform marriages and religious ceremonies. The annual Brahmostavam Festival is being celebrated on Chitra Suddah Pournima (Usually in April) attracts huge congregation.

(e) Pennaahobilam: This place situated at a distance of 35 kms. from Anantapur is an uninhabited village known for its Temple of "Sri Lakshmi Narasimha Swamy" popularly called as "Degurla Narasimha Swamy". This place is an important pilgrim centre in the District and the Car Festival on the fifth day of the dark fortnight in the month of Vaisakam (April-May) will be largely attended by devotees even from the neighbouring districts and the Karnataka

State. The temple is constructed on a hillock of 30 feet height. The main shrine consists of gigantic foot mark of 5□x3□, believed to be the foot print of Lord Narasimha. Vows are fulfilled and marriages and tonsure ceremonies are performed frequently at this shrine. The temple of Lakshmi, the lords consort is situated by the side of the main shrine. There is a spring channel in the temple known as *'Bugga Koneru'*.

(f) Puttaparthy: This village is on the banks of Chitravathi situated at a distance of about 29 kms. from Penukonda. It is the abode of Puttaparthy Sri Sathya Sai Baba, drawing devoted disciples from all over the world. There is Prasanthi Nilayam (an Ashram) constructed by the devotees. The Baba is credited with acute powers. On Sivarathri, on the birth day of the Baba and particularly during Dussehra, quite a large number of devotees visit the place.

A beautiful mantapa by name 'Poornachandra' is constructed in which a large number of Baba devotees would assemble and perform "Bhajana" on festival days.

Population

Anantapur district is second largest district in Andhra Pradesh. The district is sparsely populated. The population of rural and urban to the total population of the district works out to be 75 per cent and 25 per cent (2001 Census) as against 87.5 per cent of 1991 Census. There are 958 Females per 1000 Males (2001 Census).

The working force in the total population of district forms 48.83 per cent as per 2001 census, out of which 26 per cent are in the Agriculture Sector. The work participation rate for female is 39.4 and for male 57.8. Agriculture labour constitute main work force (37.7 per cent). Agriculture labour is the mainstay for women workers (54.5).

The district has low sex ratio, only 958 females per thousand males. It is further lower in the case of Scheduled

Castes and Scheduled Tribe Population. The overall literacy rate in the district is only 56.13 per cent and for rural areas it is much lower it is only 44.63. (*See table 3.7 and 3.8*)

Table 3.7. Population Characteristics of Anantapur District

Sl. No.	Item	Unit	
1	Population	Lakhs	36.40
	Males	Lakhs	18.59
	Females	Lakhs	17.81
2	Rural Population	Lakhs	27.21
3	Urban Population	Lakhs	9.19
4	Urban Population as % to Total	%	25.23
5	Population of Scheduled Castes	%	14.14
6	Population of Scheduled Tribes	%	3.5
7	Population (0-6)		479853
8	Sex-ratio	No	958
9	Sex-ratio (0-6)	No	959
10	Sex-ratio S.C.	No	956
11	Sex-ratio S.T.	No	935
12	No. of Households	No	779052
13	Household size	No	5.0
14	Literacy Rate		56.13
	Males		68.4
	Females		43.3
15	Revenue Divisions	No	3
16	Revenue Mandals	No	63
17	Total Number of Villages	No	3322

Source: 1. Hand Book of Anantapur District Statistics, Anantapur, 2002-03.

2. Census of India, 2001.

Table 3.8. Work Participation of Anantapur District

Sl. No.	Item	Unit	Persons	Male	Female
1	Total Workers	No	1777536	1075456	702080
2	Proportion of Non-workers	%	51.2	42.2	60.6
4	Main Workers	%	40.4	52.3	28.0
5	Marginal Workers	%	8.4	5.6	11.4
	Proportion to Total Workers				
	Cultivators	%	29.8	32.3	25.9
6	Agricultural Labour	%	37.7	26.8	54.5
	Household Industry	%	5.7	5.6	6.0
	Other Workers	%	26.7	35.3	13.6
7	Work Participation Rate	%	48.8	57.8	39.4

Source: 1. Hand Book of Anantapur District Statistics, Anantapur, 2002-03.

2. Census of India, 2001.

SECTION II

Profile of Study Villages and Mandals

The present study is carried out in 17 villages spread in ten revenue Mandals of the Anantapur and Kurnool districts. Of the 17 villages selected for the study, two villages are Municipalities, eight villages are revenue villages and seven villages are hamlet villages. The population size of these villages ranges from 407 persons to 117103 persons. Most of these villages are located in remote part of the districts. The details of nature of villages are shown in tables 3.9 and 3.12.

The study villages represent ten revenue mandals. They are Pamidi, Guntakal(M), Kalyanadurgam, Mudigubba, Puttaparthy, Yemmiganur(M), Kodumur, Mahanandi, Peapully, Bandi Atmakur mandals. These mandals are located in remote and isolate part of the districts. They are relatively small in area and are more backward mandals.

Table 3.9. Population Characteristics of the Study Area in Anantapur District

Sl No.	Name of the Village	Population	S.C Popul-ation	S.T Popul-	No.of House-holds	House size	Literates	Male	Female	Litera-cyrate
1	Anantapur	3640478	514896	127161	779052	4.7	1774088	1104042	670046	56.1
2	Guntakal	117103	16798	2046	22962	5.1	74136	43012	31124	71.4
3	Pamidi	49292	6384	2746	10302	4.8	22886	14119	8767	53.9
4	Emampuram	652	148	27	135	4.8	175	122	53	30.8
5	Kalyanadurgam	29266	2062	557	5719	5.1	17660	10112	7548	69.8
6	Uppuvanka	2588	340	69	514	5.0	1224	782	442	54.9
7	Mudigubba	58212	5774	7059	13894	4.2	26691	17221	9470	51.9
8	Mangalamadaka	3164	274	1312	758	4.2	1664	1083	581	59.3
9	Puttaparty	50091	5769	3353	11784	4.3	24826	15443	9383	56.6

Source: 1. Hand Book of Anantapur District Statistics, Anantapur, 2002-03.

2. Census of India, 2001.

Table 3.10. Work participation in the study area in Anantapur District

Name of the Village	Total Workers	Cultiv-ators %	Agricu-ltaral Labour %	House hold %	Other Work-ers %
Anantapur	1777536	29.8	37.7	5.7	26.7
Guntakal	36528	2.4	15.0	3.4	79.3
Pamidi	25567	32.1	39.6	6.9	23.0
Emampuram	400	26.5	64.3	5.0	4.5
Kalyanadurgam	9986	3.1	15.1	4.7	77.1
Uppuvanka	1451	41.4	51.6	2.6	4.4
Mudigubba	32176	43.4	39.3	3.0	14.4
Mangalamadaka	1788	51.5	41.4	1.2	5.9
Puttaparty	23956	28.1	41.8	4.4	25.7

Source: 1. Hand Book of Anantapur District Statistics, Anantapur, 2002-03.
2. Census of India, 2001.

SECTION III

Yerukulas: Socio-economic Conditions

Social Structure : Yerukulas are identified as Scheduled tribe in Andhra Pradesh. The Yerukulas traditionally represent several occupational pursuits and generally divided on the basis of occupational colonies (Thurstin 1909; Haimendorf 1943; S.S.Shashi 1995.) The Yerukulas under study as many as four such groups. These are Dabba Yerukula (48.7%) Kunchepu Yerukula (27.3%) Yettapula Yerukula /Eeta Yerukula (19%) and Nulaka Yerukula.Thus Rayalaseema Yerukulas are predominantly represented by dabba Yerukula followed by Kunchepu Yerukula and Eeta Yerukula.

Table 3.11. Population Characteristics of the Study Area in Kurnool District

Sl No.	Name of the Village	Population	S.C Popul-ation	S.T Popul-ation	No.of House-holds	House size	Literates	Male	Female	Litera-cyrate %
1	Kurnool	3529494	628637	69635	699191	5.0	1592172	1003659	588513	53.2
2	Yemmiganur	76411	7444	775	13781	5.5	36961	22859	14102	56.9
3	Parlapalli	4240	826	39	773	5.5	1161	873	288	33.8
4	Kodumur	68395	10430	544	13027	5.3	30443	19830	10613	52.7
5	Gorantla	5235	643	172	968	5.4	1809	1339	470	40.7
6	Mahanandhi	33572	6677	1656	7316	4.6	14159	9309	4850	49.6
7	Peapully	67080	8218	2558	13461	5.0	28005	18447	9558	48.7
8	Rangapuram	407	12	127	76	5.4	130	79	51	39.5
9	B.Atmakur	43988	8903	2086	10177	4.3	19327	12519	6808	51.3
10	Yerukula Colony	1499	400	286	337	4.4	646	438	208	50.6

Source: 1. Hand Book of Kurnool District Statistics, Kurnool, 2002-03.

2. Census of India, 2001.

Table 3.12 Work Participation in the Study Area in Kurnool District

Sl. No.	Name of the Village	Total Workers	Cultiv-ators %	Agricu-ltaral Labour %	House hold Indus-try %	Other Work-ers %
1	Kurnool	1745220	22.2	46.0	3.5	28.3
2	Yemmiganur	32563	3.0	32.8	14.5	49.8
3	Parlapalli	2537	35.8	56.8	1.4	60
4	Kodumur	36184	17.4	56.5	9.4	16.8
5	Gorantla	2942	15.5	74	0.9	9.4
6	Mahanandhi	18010	19.4	52.8	8.3	19.6
7	Peapully	36465	35.2	45.0	4.0	15.8
8	Rangapuram	241	37.3	33.6	9.5	19.5
9	B.Atmakur	24919	23.1	58.0	5.9	13.1
10	Yerukula Colony	908	17.8	8.6	64.8	8.8

Source: 1. Hand Book of Kurnool District Statistics, Kurnool, 2002-03.
2. Census of India, 2001.

The Yerukulas under reference belongs to nuclear families (97.7%) the practice of joint families (2.3%) (S.S.Shashi 1995; V.Lalita 1995; Thurston 1909; Bose, N.K.1971) rare among Yerukulas under reference claimed to belong Hindu religion. Yerukulas traditionally speak a dilect known as Kurru basha However our study revels that at present (G_3, G_4 generations) the Yerukulas speak in local language namely Telugu.

Socio-economic Characteristics

The socio-economic status is explained with reference to demographic, Socio and economic variables. The demographic variables refer to respondent's age, marital status, size of family, type of family. The social status variables refer to religion, mother toung, education, voter card, social participation, possession of ration card. Economic variables refer to occupation, income, land ownership, ownership of house and type of house and possession of assets.

Further an attempt is made to assess the Standard of living of the respondents. For this purpose an Index of standard of living is constructed. The standard of living of Yerukulas is understood and measured by adopting two approaches. The first approach is by eliciting the respondent's perception with regard to the standard of living experienced in different generations; the second approach is by measuring the standard of living through an Index of standard of living.

Demographic Status of Yerukulas

The study sample comprises 300 Yerukula households. The study was carried out during the years. The respondent is the head of the household. Our study revels that of the 300 hundred respondents, 97.7 per cent are male members 2.3 per cent are female members.

The *marital status* of the respondent reveals that 88.3 per cent are married; 2.3 per cent are widower; 0.7 per cent is divorcees.

The total *population size* of the study sample, including the respondent was 1415 members; of which 767 members were males and 648 members were females. The *sex ratio* of Yerukula under reference was found to be 826 women per thousand males. The sex ratio shows the lower status of Yerukula women. The sex ratio is very much less than. National (933) State (978) levels. The Yerukula population of the study sample represents three generations *viz;* G_2 generation (5 per cent) G_3 generation (59.3 per cent) and G_4

generation (81.3 per cent). The children below five years age constitute 9.03 per cent to the total Yerukula population. (Table 3.13).

Table 3.13. Population Distribution of Study Sample

Sl.No.		Male	Female	Total
1	Respondents	293	7	300
		97.7%	2.3	100%
2	Family members G2			5.00%
3	G3			59.3%
4	G4			8.14
		767	648	1415

Age: Our analysis reveals that the average age of respondent at the time of data collection was 45.16 years. The youngest member of the sample was found to be 25 years old. The oldest respondent was 68 years old. Our data revels that a large percent (65.3 per cent) of the respondent belong to middle age groups (31 to 50 years). A small percentage (2.3 percent) are above the age of 60 years 10.5 per cent of respondent under reference for found to be below 30 years age group. (See table 3.14).

Economic status

Income: Our study shows that a large majority (72 per cent) of the Yerukula respondent's annual income ranges between Rs. 6000 to Rs. 12000. 18.3 per cent of the respondent annually earn between Rs. 3000 to 6000. A small percentage (7.7 per cent) of Yerukulas were found to earn less than 3000 thousand rupees per annum. Thus our study shows that prepondering majority (98 per cent) of the Yerukulas is poor and poorest of the poor (26 per cent). The lowest income earned was found to be Rs 2000 per annum and the highest was Rs 60,000. The average income was found to be

Rs 7,428.70 with Standard deviation of Rs 5,206.65. *(Table 3.15 and 3.16).*

Table 3.14. Distribution of Respondents Age and Size of family

Age	Size of family				Total
	0 - 2	3-5	6-8	9 above	
0 - 30	3 9.7%	28 90.3%	0 0.0%	0 0.0%	31 100.0%
31-40	0 .0%	55 87.3%	8 12.7%	0 0.0%	63 100.0%
41-50	4 3.0%	105 78.9%	24 18.0%	0 0.0%	133 100.0%
51-60	7 10.6%	32 48.5%	26 39.4%	1 1.5%	66 100.0%
61 above	0 0.0%	1 14.3%	6 85.7%	0 0.0%	7 100.0%
Total	**14** **4.7%**	**221** **73.7%**	**64** **21.3%**	**1** **.3%**	**300** **100.0%**

Occupation : The Yerukulas are found to be involved in eight broad occupational categories such as profession, white collar, skilled, semi-skilled business, cultivation, Agriculture labour, (rural labour) traditional occupation. (the occupational categories are explained in detail in next chapter). A large majority of the respondent (58 per cent) were found to be involved in traditional occupations like basket weaving, pig rearing etc, agriculture labour constitute 14.3 per cent 9 per cent of Yerukula respondent are found to be involved in cultivation. Very small percentages of responds were found to be involved in professional (1.3 per cent), white collar (0.7 per cent), and skilled (0.3 per cent), 9 per cent is involved in business and semi-skilled occupations.

Table 3.15. Distribution of Respondents Age and Income

Age	Income					Total
	0 - 3000	3001- 6000	6001- 12000	12001- 18000	30001- 60000	
0 - 30	0	1	30	0	0	31
	.0%	3.2%	96.8%	.0%	.0%	100.0%
31-40	0	1	60	0	2	63
	.0%	1.6%	95.2%	.0%	3.2%	100.0%
41-50	0	17	112	2	2	133
	.0%	12.8%	84.2%	1.5%	1.5%	100.0%
51-60	16	36	14	0	0	66
	24.2%	54.5%	21.2%	.0%	.0%	100.0%
61 above	7	0	0	0	0	7
	100.0%	.0%	.0%	.0%	.0%	100.0%
Total	**23**	**55**	**216**	**2**	**4**	**300**
	7.7%	**18.3%**	**72.0%**	**.7%**	**1.3%**	**100.0%**

Land Ownership

Our data reveals that respondent below the age of 40 years, were found to be involved in modern occupational categories and constitute 10.3 per cent. On the other hand, a large percentage of respondents (60.3 per cent) were found to be 40 years above old. These members were found to be involved in traditional occupations (42 per cent), agriculture labour (12.3 per cent), and cultivation (6 per cent). In other words, it may be said that the older members have a greater leaning towards traditional occupations, and the younger are inclined towards modern occupations. These leanings, it is observed, made a difference in their earnings. The poorest of the poor (0-6000) constitute 25.3 per cent to the total respondent and were found to be involved in traditional occupations like basket weaving, pig rearing, and agriculture labour. High majority (80.3 per cent) were found to be landless. Only 19.7 per cent of the respondents were found to be having

Table 3.16. Distribution of Respondents Income and Occupations

Income	Respondent occupation								Total
	Profe-ssion	White -collar	Skilled	Busi-ness	Semi-skilled	Cultiv-ation	Agriculture laboure	Tradi-tional	
0 - 3000	0	0	0	0	0	0	18	5	23
	0.0%	0.0%	0.0%	0.0%	0.0%	0.0%	78.3%	21.7%	100.0%
3001-6000	0	0	0	2	0	1	5	47	55
	0.0%	0.0%	0.0%	3.6%	.0%	1.8%	9.1%	85.5%	100.0%
6001-12000	2	0	1	23	24	26	19	121	216
	.9%	.0%	.5%	10.6%	11.1%	12.0%	8.8%	56.0%	100.0%
12001-18000	1	0	0	0	0	0	1	0	2
	50.0%	0.0%	0.0%	0.0%	0.0%	0.0%	50.0%	.0%	100.0%
30001-60000	1	2	0	0	0	0	0	1	4
	25.0%	50.0%	0.0%	0.0%	0.0%	0.0%	0.0%	25.0%	100.0%
	4	**2**	**1**	**25**	**24**	**27**	**43**	**174**	**300**
Total	**1.3%**	**.7%**	**.3%**	**8.3%**	**8.0%**	**9.0%**	**14.3%**	**58.0%**	**100.0%**

Table 3.17. Distribution of Respondents by Age and Occupation

Age	Respondent								Total
	Profession	White-collar	Skilled	Business	Semi-skilled	Cultivation	Agriculture labour	Traditional	
0 - 30	2	0	0	3	11	1	1	13	31
	6.5%	.0%	.0%	9.7%	35.5%	3.2%	3.2%	41.9%	100.0%
31-40	1	1	1	4	8	8	5	35	63
	1.6%	1.6%	1.6%	6.3%	12.7%	12.7%	7.9%	55.6%	100.0%
41-50	1	1	0	17	5	16	18	75	133
	.8%	.8%	.0%	12.8%	3.8%	12.0%	13.5%	56.4%	100.0%
51-60	0	0	0	1	0	2	13	50	66
	.0%	.0%	.0%	1.5%	.0%	3.0%	19.7%	75.8%	100.0%
61 above	0	0	0	0	0	0	6	1	7
	.0%	.0%	.0%	.0%	.0%	.0%	85.7%	14.3%	100.0%
Total	**4**	**2**	**1**	**25**	**24**	**27**	**43**	**174**	**300**
	1.3%	**.7%**	**.3%**	**8.3%**	**8.0%**	**9.0%**	**14.3%**	**58.0%**	**100.0%**

some land holdings. Most of them have marginal holdings. The highest holding was found to be nine acres.

Our data shows that large majorities of the yerukulas landless (80.3%) it appears majority of the Yerukulas were neither considered over benefited by the land assignment programme. A small percentage however, own land (19.7%) most of these members are marginal farmers. The largest land owner owns nine acres of land. It is observed that these owners of the land are involved in various occupational pursuits. (*Table 3.17 and 3.18*)

Table 3.18. Distribution of Occupation and Land Ownership

	Own land		Total
	Yes	No	
Profession	2 50.0%	2 50.0%	4 100.0%
White collar	0 .0%	2 100.0%	2 100.0%
Skilled	0 .0%	1 100.0%	1 100.0%
Business	7 28.0%	18 72.0%	25 100.0%
Semi-skilled	1 4.2%	23 95.8%	24 100.0%
Cultivation	22 81.5%	5 18.5%	27 100.0%
Agriculture labour	3 7.0%	40 93.0%	43 100.0%
Traditional	24 13.8%	150 86.2%	174 100.0%
Total	**59** **19.7%**	**241** **80.3%**	**300** **100.0%**

House and Type of House: It is found that 34.33 percentage of respondents own house. It is further observed that the pucca houses constitute 23.3 percentages. (*Table 3.19*)

Table 3.19. Respondent Occupation and House

	Respondent house		Total
	Yes	No	
Profession	4	0	4
	100.0%	.0%	100.0%
White collar	2	0	2
	100.0%	.0%	100.0%
Skilled	1	0	1
	100.0%	.0%	100.0%
Business	25	0	25
	100.0%	.0%	100.0%
Semi-skilled	17	7	24
	70.8%	29.2%	100.0%
Cultivation	27	0	27
	100.0%	.0%	100.0%
Agriculture labour	33	10	43
	76.7%	23.3%	100.0%
Traditional	165	9	174
	94.8%	5.2%	100.0%
Total	**274**	**26**	**300**
	91.3%	**8.7%**	**100.0%**

Assets: Our data study shows that 32.6 per cent respondent's pigs and movable, 34.3 per cent respondent were immovable, only 13.6 per cent respondents costly items received. *(See Table 3.20 on next page)*

Ration card: Our study shows that 15.7 per cent do not possess ration cards (public distribution system). The larger percentage that were denied ration cards were among those respondents who are below 30 years of age and those who are above 61 years of age.

Vote: Our data shows that 20 per cent of respondents did not have voting right because they did not have proper identification.

Table 3.20. Distribution of Occupation and Assets

	Assets		Total
	Yes	No	
Profession	1	3	4
	25.0%	75.0%	100.0%
White collar	0	2	2
	.0%	100.0%	100.0%
Skilled	1	0	1
	100.0%	.0%	100.0%
Business	13	12	25
	52.0%	48.0%	100.0%
Semi-skilled	9	15	24
	37.5%	62.5%	100.0%
Cultivation	26	1	27
	96.3%	3.7%	100.0%
Agriculture labour	32	11	43
	74.4%	25.6%	100.0%
Traditional	130	44	174
	74.7%	25.3%	100.0%
Total	**212**	**88**	**300**
	70.7%	**29.3%**	**100.0%**

Social Status

All the Yerukala families under the reference are observed to practice Hindu religious practices. None of the Yerukula families under reference were confined in the rehabitation settlements sponsored by the British Government and the Christian Missionaries during pre-independence period. They have reported Telugu language as their mother toung. Of the 300 families under reference 15.7 per cent do not possesses ration cards (public distribution system). In other words these families are deprived of food-security and denied social identity and security; as ration card is considered as both as an identity and social security card for various purposes to avail Government sponsored facilities and benefits; including voter cards. The larger percentage who were denied ration cards (white cards) were among those respondents who are below 30 years of age (32.3%); and those who are above 61 years of age (28.6%) *(See Table 3.21.)*

Table 3.21 Distribution of Respondents Age and Ration card

Age	Ration card		Total
	Yes	No	
0 - 30	21	10	31
	67.7%	32.3%	100.0%
31-40	56	7	63
	88.9%	11.1%	100.0%
41-50	113	20	133
	85.0%	15.0%	100.0%
51-60	58	8	66
	87.9%	12.1%	100.0%
61above	5	2	7
	71.4%	28.6%	100.0%
Total	**253**	**47**	**300**
	84.3%	**15.7%**	**100.0%**

Universal adult franchise is the right of every citizen of India. This right, granted by the Republic of India ensured, Social equality and social inclusiveness of every section of India's population. Therefore, the exercise of this right is indicative of social status of individuals in terms of social exclusion and inclusiveness. Our data reveals that 20 per cent of Yerukala respondents did not vote as they did not have proper identification. Those who could not vote represent all adult age groups under reference *(the details are presented in Table 3.22).*

Table 3.22. Distribution of Respondents Age and Voting Behavior

Age	voted		Total
	Yes	No	
0 - 30	27	4	31
	87.1%	12.9%	100.0%
31-40	47	16	63
	74.6%	25.4%	100.0%
41-50	112	21	133
	84.2%	15.8%	100.0%
51-60	49	17	66
	74.2%	25.8%	100.0%
61above	5	2	7
	71.4%	28.6%	100.0%
Total	**240**	**60**	**300**
	80.0%	**20.0%**	**100.0%**

Education is one important social variable which indicates social status of different communities. Our data shows that large majorities of the Yerukula respondent are illiterate, however the gratifying factor is that the percentage of illiterates is less than 13 per cent among the younger respondent who are below the age group of 15-30 years. Illiteracy among Yerukula respondent is found to be directly propositional to age. In other words higher the age group, greater the illiteracy percentage.

Among the Yerukula respondents 18.7 per cent have studied up to upper primary level and only 5 per cent have studied up to higher secondary level and above level *(See Table 3.23 on next page).*

Social Participation

Participation in social functions, attaining social positions and restriction on social participation are indicators of a community's social status. Our study shows that only 4.7 per cent of the respondents have held any position as office

Table 3.23. Distribution of Respondents by Age and Education

Age	Education						Total
	Illiterate	Primary	Upper primary	High school	10+2	College	
0 - 30	4	6	12	7	1	1	31
	12.9%	19.4%	38.7%	22.6%	3.2%	3.2%	100.0%
31-40	44	13	4	0	1	1	63
	69.8%	20.6%	6.3%	.0%	1.6%	1.6%	100.0%
41-50	109	16	4	3	1	0	133
	82.0%	12.0%	3.0%	2.3%	.8%	.0%	100.0%
51-60	65	0	1	0	0	0	66
	98.5%	.0%	1.5%	.0%	.0%	.0%	100.0%
61	7	0	0	0	0	0	7
above	100.0%	.0%	.0%	.0%	.0%	.0%	100.0%
Total	**229**	**35**	**21**	**10**	**3**	**2**	**300**
	76.3%	**11.7%**	**7.0%**	**3.3%**	**1.0%**	**.7%**	**100.0%**

bearers. Only 23.7 per cent have political party affiliations. Majority of the respondents (62.7%) reported that they freely participate in social functions. 37.3 per cent reported that they do not participate in social functions. However, only 3 per cent reported that they experience social restrictions *(See Table 3.24)*.

Table 3.24. Social Exclusions & Inclusions Identity & Social participation

	Ration card	Voted	Participation	Social Resections	Political party affiliated	Social positions
Yes	253	240	188	9	71	14
	84.3%	80.0%	62.7%	3.0%	23.7%	4.7%
No	47	60	112	291	229	286
	15.7%	20%	37.3%	97.0%	76.3%	95.3%

Standard of Living

The index of standard of living comprises five indicators such as *Annual Income, Livelyhood, Food Security, Housing*, and *Assets*. Each indicator comprises five items. These items are arranged in a graded manner ranging from low to high. Accordingly weighted scores are assigned from one to five. The details are as under.

Annual Incomes are graded 0-3000, 3000-6000, 6000-12000, 12000-18000, and 18000 above. The income eighteen thousand above is considered above poverty line and assigned score of five.

The indicator livelyhood comprises five items such as very unstable livelyhood, unstable livelyhood, seasonal livelyhood, stable livelyhoods and very stable livelyhoods. Livelyhoods are graded as very unstable livelyhood to very stable livelyhood. The criterion for stability is based on the duration of employment availability for livelyhood in a year. A very unstable livelyhood includes livelyhood practices such as thieving, dacoit, and hunting. Unstable livelyhood practices comprise semi-skilled practices like tractor driving, Auto-rickshaw driving and other odd jobs; Seasonal livelyhoods include marginal labour including agriculture, construction labour, commission agency, cultivation. Stable livelyhood practices include split bamboo basket weaving, pig rearing, moneylending etc. Very stable occupations are salaried occupations.

Food security is graded on the basis of consumption and non-consumption of meals, as it was easy to recall the memory. Food security indicators comprises five items such—often starved; often hungry; food was scares; not misers meals; meals twice or thrice a day. Often starved in a week was assigned lowest score. Consumption of meals twice or thrice a day is assigned highest score of five. The quality and the quantity of the meals, however, were not considered due to lack of proper response. Hence, food security is determined by the frequency of meals consumed in a week.

Housing was judged on the basis of the type of dwelling they lived in. The indicators comprises five items such as—shack, hut, kutcha house, semi-pucca house and pucca house. Accordingly pucca houses are given highest score of five; shack was given lowest score of one.

Assets are graded based on their possessions. Those who did not have any assets are given lowest score of one, those who possess one or two milch cattle, fowls, sheep or pigs or rare pigs are given a score of two. In addition to the livestock those who possess bicycle rickshaw, radio etc, and movable assets are assigned a score of three. In addition to livestock and movable assets those who possess immovable assets like farmland, house site or house are given a score of four. Those who own costly items like gold, motor cycle etc, in addition to livestock and movable assets are given a score of five.

The composite index of standard of living comprises a maximum score of (25) and a minimum score of five (5). The index is graded in to five categories. Such as very bad, (>5), bad (6-10), not so bad (11-15 good enough 16-20 satisfactory 21-25). The responds are appraised about the details of indicators before eliciting their perception on standard of living experienced in different generation. The assessment is based on respondents actual living conditions experienced at the time of study.

The index of standard of living reveals that 19.4 per cent of the respondent's standard of living can be considered as satisfactory 31 per cent of responds standard of livings is good enough 28.3 per cent respondents standard of living is not so bad 19.4 per cent of responds experience bad standard of living very bad standard of living consistence only 1.8 per cent.

61 per cent of the respondents experience *satisfactory* levels of *food security* 81.33 per cent respondents have *good enough* opportunity for livelihood. 73.33 per cent of respondents earn annual income which is not so bad 56.66 per cent of the respondent's dwellings are bad. Which are only huts 34.33 per cent own some assets of movable property like pigs, bicycle etc., *(these details of presented in table 3.25).*

Table 3.25. Index of Standard Living

Items	Very bad	Bad	Not so Bad	Good enough	Satisf-actory	Total
	1	2	3	4	5	6
Food security	-	3 1.0%	4	110 33.66%	183 61.3%	300
Lively-hood	-	14	36	244 81.33%	6	300
Income	14	60	220 73.33%	2	4	300
Housing	-	170 56.66%	67	6	57	300
Assets	14	44	98	103 34.33%	41	300
Total	**28** **5.6**	**291** **58.2**	**425** **85**	**465** **93**	**291** **58.2**	**1500** **300**
%	**1.8**	**19.4**	**28.3**	**31.0**	**19.4**	**100%**

Table 3.26. Respondents perception of Standard of Living

Items	No	%
Very Bad	3	1.0
Bad	82	27.3
Not So Bad	173	57.7
Good Enough	11	3.7
Satisfactory	31	10.3
Total	**300**	**100**

However, the respondent's perception about the standard of living is slightly different from the objective assessment. Only 10.3 per cent of the respondents consider that their standard of living is satisfactory. Similarly 57.7 per cent of the respondents consider their standard of living is not so bad. However 27.3 per cent and 1 per cent of respondents respectively consider there standard of living is bad and very bad. The factors which promoted these negative perceptions are poor housing conditions lack of assets and poor incomes *(See Table 3.26).*

REFERENCES

Enthoven, R.E., *"The Tribes and Castes of Bombay"*, (Bombay: Government of Central Press 1922), Vol. II, p. 267.

Furar, C.V., Haimendorf, *"The Tribes of India, The Struggle of Survival"*, Oxford University Press, Delhi, 1982.

Hassan, S.S. 1920. *'Castes and Tribes of the H.E.H. The Nizam's Dominions Hyderabad State'*, The Times Press, Bombay.

Hand Book of Kurnool District Statistics, Kurnool, 2002-03.

Hand Book of Kurnool District Statistics, Anantapur, 2002-03.

Lalitha, V., *"The Making of Criminal Tribes," Pattern and Transition,* New Era Publication Madras, 1995.

Meena Radha Krsihna, "The Criminal Tribe Act in Madras Presidency," Implication for Itinerant Trading Communities, *The Indian Economic and Social History Review,* 26, 3, Sage, New Delhi 1989.

Mohan Rao, K., *"Tribes of Andhra Pradesh,"* 1998, TCR, and TI, Hyderabad.

Shashi S.S. *"Tribes of Andhra Pradesh"* Anmol Publication Pvt. Ltd; New Delhi, 1995.

Registrar General, *Census of India,* New Delhi 2001.

Pratap, D.R. 1982. *'Approach to Tribal Development',* in Buddadeb Chaudhury (ed): *Tribal Development in India.* New Delhi: Inter India Publication.

Singh,K.S. 1998. *'India's Communities',* Oxford University Press, New Delhi.

Subba Ramaraju, Sudhakar,C. *Developmental Programmes and Social Transfermation.* Associated Publishers, New Delhi-2006.

Sen Amrty, 2000. *Social Exclusion: Concept Application and Scrutiny.* Office of Environment and Social Development, Asian Development Bank.

Shashi S.S. *"Tribes of Andhra Pradesh"* Anmol Publication Pvt. Ltd; New Delhi, 1995.

Sareen, H.K. 1980. *Insurgency in North-East: A Study of Sino-American Role.* New Delhi; Sterling Publishers.

Sen, J. 1969. The Jharkhand Movement', *Seminar on the Tribal Situation in India.* Shimla: Indian Institute of Advanced Study.

Sengupta, N. 1980. 'Caste and Tribals in Jharkandh', *Economic and Political Weekly,* 15(14): 664-71.

Thruston, E., 1909. *'Castes and Tribes of Southern India'* Madras: Government Press, Madras; rpt. 1975, Cosmo Publications, Delhi), Vol. II, pp. 284-295.

Thruston, E., 1909. *'Castes and Tribes of Southern India'* Madras: Government Press, Madras; rpt. 1975; Cosmo Publications, Delhi), Vol. VI, pp. 292-325.

Thruston, E., *Castes and Tribes of Southern India* (Madras: Government Press, 1090; rpt. 1975, Delhi; Cosmo Publications), Vol. I.

Umamohan, C, Naganna, A., "Yerukula Tribes and Social Transformation," Bharatiya Adimajathi Sevak Sangh (*Vanyagati*), New Delhi 2006.

Umamohan, C. A.Naganna, Globalisation: Continuity and Change of Livelihood and Interdependence: A Study of Yerukula Tribe (*paper submitted at the National Seminar on Globalisation: Indian Society,* Continuities and Change Hyderabad, 7th April, 2006).

Umamohan, C. A.Naganna, Occupational Changes and Mobility: An Intra- Generational Study of Yerukulas in Rayalaseema Region of AP. *National Seminar on 3rd and 4th November, 2006.* Dravidian University, Kuppam.

Umamohan, C. A.Naganna, Reproductive Healthcare An Inter-Generational Study of Yerukulas in Rayalaseema Region of AP. *National Seminar on 3rd and 4th November, 2006,* Dravidian University, Kuppam.

Umamohan, C. A.Naganna, Perception and Assessment on Standard of Living, Quality of Life and Social Well-being: An Inter-generational Study of a Stigmatised Scheduled Tribe the Yerukulas in Rayalaseema Region of Andhra

Pradesh *National Seminar on Tribal Development: A Myth or Pragmatic Reality?* 26th and 27th February, 2007. Organised by Department of Anthropology Sri Venkateswara University, Tirupati.

Umamohan, C. A.Naganna, Social Stigma and Yerukula Tribe: A Study of Social Exclusion and Inclusion. *Paper presented to the International Seminar Social Exclusion and Inclusive Policies* In South Asia 17th to 19th March, 2008, Shivaji University, Kolhapur.

Umamohan, C. A.Naganna, Educational Attainments and Empowerment of A Stigmatised Scheduled Tribe: An Intergenerational Study of Yerukula Tribe in Rayalaseema. *Paper presented to the National Seminar, Education and Social Empowerment,* 5th and 6th July 2007, Dr. B. R. A. Open University, Hyderabad

Naganna, A. Globalisation, Education and Occupational Changes: A Study of Stigmatised Scheduled Tribe—The Yerukulas. *Paper presented Workshop for Young Social Scientists,* 5 and 6 October. Jammu University

Umamohan, C. A.Naganna, Social Stigma and Social Exclusion: A Study of Yerukula Tribe in Rayalaseema Region of Andhra Pradesh. *Paper presented to the National Workshop, Social Exclusion and Inclusive Policy with Special Reference to Weaker Sections of India,* 28th to 29th March, 2008 Andhra University, Visakhapatnam.

Unpublished Monograph of TCRTI, Government of Andhra Pradesh 2000 and Rural house Hold Healthcare Needs and Availability, 1992.

Workshop Proceedings (2002), Andhra Pradesh Community Forest Management Project (*Souvenir*), Forest Department, Government of Andhra Pradesh.

Chapter 4

Yerukulas
Social Exclusion and Inclusion

The present chapter attempts to examine the social transformation of the stigmatised tribe Yerukula within the conceptual framework of Social Exclusion and Inclusion.

The social transformation is examined in the context of overall developmental programmes and the constitutional commitments that have been initiated and launched in India since independence. Therefore, for this purpose of analysis the changes that have taken place in the lives of Yerukulas over a period of four generations *viz.,* Grandfather (G_1), father (G_2) Respondent (G_3) and Respondent employed son (G_4) were considered.

Further the social transformation within the conceptual framework of Social Exclusion and Inclusion of the four generations is examined with reference to changes related to.

- Livelihood opportunities
- Access to education
- Access to reproductive health
- Stigma—social exclusion and inclusion
- Standard of living
- Quality of life
- Social well-being

SECTION - I

Livelihood

In India, traditional social status and social mobility are of corporate in nature however the modern developments have ushered changes and facilitated individual mobility. In this context occupations pursued by an individual assumes importance in determining one's status and as well opportunities for social mobility. Similarly, the levels of development is also understood with reference to transition and changes in the occupational structure, *viz;* primary, secondary, territionary occupational sectors; agrarian-industrial; industrial-service.

Therefore in the present chapter an exercise is made to examine the occupational pursuits and are occupational mobility trends and changes to understand the impact of development programmes and resultant trends of social transformation.

For this purpose the analysis is presented in the following sections, *viz*: (1) the distributions of occupational pursuits; deviation from traditional occupations; Intra-generational changes in pursuits of the livelihood; Inter-generational occupational mobility trends; and stability of livelihood and inter-generational trends.

Almost one and half centuries ago, the Yerukulas were nomads and are considerable as Tribals. As such they did not have a place in rural occupational hierarchy. In rural India occupations are always associated with caste. Besides Yerukulas had a tendency of criminality and known for their coravery and adaucity. Hence, occupationally they were marginalized and socially exclusive chose such occupations / livelyhood pursuits which were caste free and allowed them to practice their criminal skills such as theieving, dacoity as well.

They made a living as basket-weaves, rope-making, mat weaving, fortune telling, snake-charms, tatto-makers, musicians, engaged in marriages, aerobatas, sellers of salt, tamarind curry-leaf and pulses (Thurston 1909),Paparao Naidu 1905, Gnthrop 1882) in the streets or villages and they were always on the move from one village to another. Apart from earning their livelihood by traditional occupations, some of them resorted to such anti-social activities like robberies, decoities and petty thefts. When the criminal behaviours of the Yerukulas become a problem for the then British Government, it felt it necessity as preventive and deterrent purposes to declare the entire tribe legally criminal. Therefore, the British Government enacted the Criminal Tribe Act of 1871with the assumption that unless the entire tribe was put under certain preventive measures and restricting it would be difficult to deter the professional criminals. (Simhadri-1979:28), marginalised livelihood pursuits, nomadic and semi-nomadic life style and stigmatic label as a criminal tribes have furthered their marginalization, social exclusion in the pursuit of livelihood. The strict police watch, established Criminal Tribe settlements, reformation rehabilitation were some of the unsucceful efforts made by the British to transform Yerukulas. However, since within the past one hundred and fifty years, the Yerukula culture and society have undergone several referable changes.

It was during the post-Independence ever, that the Yerukulas had a chance to reform their life style. The socio-economic changes in the rural areas, universal adult franchise repeal of Criminal Tribe Act (1871) relaxation of police harassment and the community development programmes have offered a chance to lead a settled and sedentary life and pursue such livelihood pursuits which are in demand for rural/ peasant markets such as bamboo basket weaving. Though the stigma of criminal tribe and the marginalisation of livelihood pursuits have continued the intensively as declining trend.

The Yerukulas, either on their own accord and an account of the efforts of the government have settled in and around the villages, semi-urban places and urban centres and pursued their traditional occupations besides adopting non-traditional ones. This brought some changes in the spheres of their social, political life. The Government of India repealed the criminal Tribe Act in 1952 and legally changed the term criminal tribes to notified tribe them to Denotified Tribe (Vimuktajatis) and finally included the Denotified Tribe under the scheduled tribe. Now the Yerukula is a Scheduled Tribe.

The enactment of Criminal Tribe Act 1871 labelled and stigmatised this people as criminal tribe. Thus they were branded with an undeniable stigma of criminal tribe. Since this act was repealed in 1952 after Independence the Yerukulas gradually assumed sedentary settled life. Most of them however pursued traditional occupations.

Yerukulas and Traditional Occupation

The traditional occupations are distinct in each of the endogamous group of Yerukulas. The endogamous Yerukula sub-groups are identified with a particular pursuit(s) and referred as such. The writings of Paparao Naidu 1905; Thurston 1909; Hussein SS 1920; Enthoven 1922; have reported the occupational endogamous and Yerukula sub-groups and their livelihood pursuits. Some of these sub-divisions are exogamous, but in their common pursuits of criminal activity (robbery or snatching away or theft), they are all identical with no distinction among them. Such were the people who were brought to the settlements and dubbed as a criminal tribe.

After Independence also some of these occupational traditions have continued. But some of the livelihood pursuits have been lost. The post Independence scenario particularly the first two decades of post Independence is reported by Shashi 1995; Lalitha 1995; K.S.Singh 1998; Simhadri 1974. (See Table 4.1)

Classifications of Yerukulas

The Yerukula are divided into three large endogamous groups on the basis of their traditional occupations. A brief portrayal of major Yerukula occupational sub groups is presented in here.

Table 4.1. Yerukuls: Endogamous sub Groups and Livelyhood/ occupations

SI.	Yerukula Endogamous sub-group	Occupations	Reported By
1	2	3	4
1	Dabba Yerukula	Split bamboo basket weaving	Paparao Naidu (1905), Thurston (1909) Shashi (1995)
2	Yeetha pulla Yerukula	Wild date palm leaves mat weaving	K.S.Singh(1998)
3	URA Yerukula	Pig rearing	K.S.Singh(1998)
4	Kunchepu yerukula	Makers of weavers comb	Shashi (1995)
5	Uppu Yerukula	Salt hawkers	K.S.Singh(1998) Lalitha(1995)
6	Karivepaku Yerukula	Hawkers of curry leaves	Thurston(1909) K.S.Singh(1998)
7	Nara Yerukula	Rope makers (with fiber)	Thurston (1909) K.S.Singh(1998)
8	Kavali Yerukula	Crop watchers	K.S.Singh(1998)
9	Yeddu Yerukula	transporters of merchandise on bullock	Thurston (1909) K.S.Singh(1998)
10	Parikamuggula Yerukula	Sooth sayers, beggars	Lalitha(1995)
11	Kothula Yerukula	Acrobats	K.S.Singh(1998)
12	Bajanthi Yerukula	Musicians and Acrobats	Lalitha(1995)
13	Kooth Yerukula	Taltooers	Lalitha(1995)
14	Thabbi Koravas	Mats,baskets,ropes, stigma,graneries	Lalitha(1995)
15	Kavalkar Koravas	Watchmen	Lalitha(1995)

...(Contd.)

1	2	3	4
16	Kallu Koravas	Mending stones and working wadde Yerukula on roads by carrying stones and mud	Lalitha(1995)
17	Gadipatti Kaikaries	Basket making	Lalitha(1995)
18	Konche Koravas	To make brushes for sale	Lalitha(1995)
19	Koot Kaikaries	Koot means dancing so they live by prostitution	Lalitha(1995)
20	Pan Kaikaries	Exhibit serpents from door to door beg	Lalitha(1995)

Bidari Yerukula: Bidari means a wandering merchant. Bidari Yerukulas traditional occupation are trading. They engaged in trade, carrying rock salt, tamarind, curry leafs (Murraya Koenigii) and pulses. They moved into the neibhbouring states like Tamilanadu and Karnataka in the south and Maharashtra in the north. In olden days these Bidari Yerukula moved from place to place with their commodities carried on the back of asses the bullocks while mentioning about the occupation of these Yerukula, Ramesan (1960) wrote:

"Before the advent of British in India, these tribes were also used by the Transport Department of the then Governments to supply cattle to the regiments in the frequent disturbances that occurred in the country. Sub-divisions of this tribe, *viz*: Kabadi owned hundreds of asses, bullocks and barren cows and utilised them in the transport of salt grain. The introduction of the Railways proved a curse to them, since their traditional job, namely transport was taken away by the Railway, and hence they had to sell away their animals and reduce themselves to abject poverty (Ramesan, 1961).

The Bidari Yerukula also engage themselves in other traditional occupational such as business, basketery, making ropes and twines from forest fibers, slings and ropes for drawing water and fathering animals. In certain places a few of them are musicians also. The Bidari Yerukula who settled in plain villages and have taken to agriculture are also referred to by other caste people as Uri Yerukula (Village Yerukula). The difference between Bidari Yerukula and Uri Yerukula is, the Uri Yerukula have forgotten completely their dialect, Yerukula basha and they are Telugu speakars, and also they think that they are culturally superior to Bidari Yerukulas, who still live in remote ares with traditional wandery trade.

Dabba Yerukula: Dabba means bamboosticks. They are called Dabba Yerukula, because this groups prepars baskets, thattis and cradles from bamboo sticks. They are mostly nomadic. But now-a-days some of them have settled in towns.

Kunchi Yerukula: Kunchi, means brush, their main occupation is pig-rearing preparation of kunchelu (long big brushes used by local weavers for preparing the warp) and selling them. This group is otherwise, known as Gadde Yerukula, as their women are engaged in gadde or sodi, *i.e.,* fortune-telling. Their women generally go about the streets, calling out Yeruko, Amma Yeruku, *i.e.,* prophecies, mother, prophecies. These groups of Yerukula also prepare baskets and childrens toys out of the Palmyrah leaves. A few of them are also beggars. Though this group is also nomadic in nature, some of them are found to have settled permanently in some places. Under this group, three other Yerukula groups are included; these are Jakkala Yerukula, Pamula Yerukula and Kothula Yerukula.

Jakkala Yerukula: Women of this group are proficient in tattooing and they move from place to place to earn their livelihood. Males rear pigs and sell pigs and pig manure. They are also called Parik Muggulavalu.

Pamula Yerukula: This group is also nomadic and they catch snakes. These people are in the habit of performing magic locally known as modi. They are also called as 'Pedditigolla varu'

Kothula Yerukula: This section of families is engaged in making the monkeys perform aerobatic. Hence, they were called Kothula Yerukula.

Occupational Distribution and changes: The Twenty first Century Scenario

The Yerukula respondents under reference have reported that they are distributed in as many as twenty one different occupational pursuits. Most of which are traditional ones. It is also observed that majority are involved in more than one pursuit. The livelyhood pursuits are presented in table 4.2.

Table 4.2. Respondents occupational Distributions

S.No.	Item	No
1.	Teacher	4
2.	Bank clerk	1
3.	Bus conductor	1
4.	Bus driver	1
5.	Mango commission agent	5
6.	Moneylending	8
7.	Petty business	6
8.	Arrack dealers	6
9.	Auto driver	11
10.	Tractor driver	11
11.	Tailor	2
12.	Cultivation	27
13.	Dry milch cattle-rearing	7
14.	Goat rearing	7
15.	Pig rearing	23
16.	Basket weaving	83
17.	Mat weaving	50
18.	Rope making	11
19.	Hunting/Begging	11
20.	Agriculture labour	27
21.	Construction labour	16
	Total	**300**

The occupations reported were classified into ten occupational categories based on their nature such as Traditional; semi skilled; cultivation; business; skilled; white collar; executive; professional; and other miscellaneous occupations agriculture labour and construction labour.

Traditionally the Yerukula communities are landless and derive their livelihood by making baskets, mat weaving, rearing pigs, herding cattle and gathering forest produce. Their women seek alms and tell fortune to the clients while playing the tambura. Some of them work as agricultural labourers. Children are engaged in rearing pigs and in making baskets. The traditional relations are restricted within the community. Their children do not attend schools since they lead a semi-nomadic life.

Traditional occupations are those occupations which are carried out owing to ascription or simply due to their involvement traditionally. These are mostly craft oriented, agrarian related and dependent on ecological and environmental resources; some of them are being practised as caste occupations by certain other castes. Basket weaving with split bamboo; Mat weaving with leaves of wild date palm; Natural fiber rope making; tending pig, goat/sheep/ dry milch cattle etc., are some of the examples.

Semi-skilled occupations are those which emerged in the recent times and are not necessarily ascriptive, they require some amount of acquired/ learned modern skills but with out legal/ authentic certificates. Tractor driving; Auto driving, tailoring are a few of such occupations. These are caste free occupations.

Cultivation is an open occupation. In an effort to reform Yerukulas some of the Yerukulas were encouraged to take up cultivation during pre-independence era and later by the State Government. Some of the Yerukulas have acquired land on their own enterprise.

Traditionally, Yerukulas were known for their trading and transport service activities, particularly before the advent or Railways in India. Even now some of them practice various business activities. The business activities include activities like commission agency; arrack dealership, petty business, moneylending etc., all these *viz*: traditional, semi skilled; cultivation and business pursuits do not require any formal training or educational attainments and are mostly either parent conferred/ascriptive by tradition.

Occupational categories such as Skilled, White collar, Executive Professions are modern occupations which require varying definite levels of educational attainment and for some certain level of formal training. These are achieved positions and are by and large secular in nature.

The different occupations pursued by the respondents are as follows: Teacher (4) which is a professional pursuit, Bank clerk (1) Bus conductor (1) are white collar positions; Bus driver (1) is skilled ones and require formal training, licence and educational attainment. All these occupations are modern and secular occupations and are achieved.

Mango garden commission agent (5) money lending (8) petty business (6) Arrack shop dealer (6) are business activities; Tractor driver, Auto divers (22), Tailor (2) are semi-skilled activities; these are partly manual too.

Dry milch cattle rearing to raise calves, goat/sheep, rearing (7); pig rearing (23); bamboo basket weaving (83); mat weaving (50); agriculture labour (27); construction labour (16); begging; hunting, rope making (11); cultivation (27). These are traditional occupations. Occupations (19).

Deviations from the Traditions Occupations

India is by and large a caste based society. The traditional occupational structure was therefore, too was caste base, as each caste was associated with a specific caste occupation. But traditionally the tribal's were not in this ambit. Yet some of the tribes have pursued certain occupations as their monopoly. The Yerukula tribal's traditional occupational pursuit was not very clear. It was reported prior to the advent of Railways the Yerukulas were involved in transport of merchandise of rock-salt in the caravans, and the means of transport was donkey. The introduction of railways deprived Yerukulas from this livelihood pursuits and thus they were forced to take-up highway robbery, dacoity, theiving (*Ramaswamy,* 1960).

And on the other hand the researchers have reported that Yerukulas were divided into occupationally endogamous sub groups. (*Thurston, Saha H.A, Lalita.V, Ghury.G.S*) This indicates Yerukulas follow certain occupational pursuits with monopoly. The Yerukula sub groups and occupations associated with them are presented in table 4.1. For the purpose of analysis of occupational deviation the researcher refers to the above mentioned occupational affiliation.

The Yerukula respondents under reference represent such occupationally endogamous groups as Dabba-Yerukula (48.7), Kunchepu Yerukula (27.3), Nulaka Yerukula (5.0), and Eeta Yerukula/Eetapulla Yerukula (19.0). Our data shows that only 58 per cent of Yerukulas have adhered to traditional callings and none of the respondents are representing such traditional occupations like making weavers komb (Kunchepu Yerukula). Very small percentage are involved in fiber rope making (nulaka) (3.67%); equally small percentage were found to be involved in mat weaving (mats made of date palm leaves) Etta pulla (16.67). A large percentage however, are involved in spilt bamboo weaving (27.67) which is considered to be the vocation of Dabba Yerukula; and not all these members belong to Dabba Yerukula group 7.6 per cent are involved in pig-rearing and 2.3 per cent are involved in dry milch cattle-rearing. A good percentage (42.00) are found to be involved in other occupations like cultivation, agriculture labour, business, auto driving, moneylending, bus driver, conductor etc.

Thus our analysis shows that in these modern days, Yerukula do not strictly adhere to their traditionally endogamous occupational callings. Further our data also shows that the Yerukula are keen to adopt *and welcome changes in their occupational* callings that would improve their levels of living. The percentage of occupation deviation irrespective of sub-group affiliation is found to be 52.00 percentages.

It is observed that at present the Yerukulas of Rayalaseema are not involved in vending, trading curry leaves, rock salt; transport services; performing modi; acrobats, or kunchelu to which they were traditionally associated and are known.

Occupational Mobility

Since the enactment of Criminal Tribes Act of 1871 in general and in particular after the repeal of the act in 1952, the Yerukulas have settled in and around the rural, semi-urban places and urban centres. They are involved in a variety of occupational pursuits. Notable among them being basket weaving, pig-rearing. The reformative efforts, constitutional safeguards and the general development and welfare efforts by the government *led to changes in the life style and occupational pursuits* of Yerukula Tribes.

The impact of the development programmes is best understood by examining changes in occupational pursuites, trends of life opportunities and stability of livelihood pursuites. Therefore in the present section on attempt is made to examine occupational changes and occupational mobility trends to understand the impact of developmental programmes. Occupational changes are examined with reference to changes from ascriptive mode of occupation to achievement oriented occupations and also movement from traditional to modern occupations.

Traditional occupations are those livelihood pursuits which are being carried out since generations by virtue of caste affiliation or sub-sect cultural affiliation, these occupations are thus parent conferred occupations or caste occupations and are thus ascriptive in nature. They do not require any formal training, qualification, or achievement. The only requirement is birth or affiliation to a certain culture Generally speaking traditional occupations are specific monopoly of certain groups. By and large traditional occupations are based on the indigenous resources and ecology, indigenous technology, manual and artisan/craft.

Modern occupations are those occupations which have emerged in the recent decades as a sequel of industrialisation technology development and modern education. These occupations are by and large free from tradition/ caste/cultural affiliation. These are achievement oriented and require some level of modern education or formal training/skills. In other words, modern occupations do not form a part of traditional agrarian occupational structure and are relatively newly created structural positions.

Occupational Mobility: The occupational distribution at the two time periods is matched through *mobility matrix* to analyse the occupational mobility trends and to calculate the *structural mobility.* The minimum amount of mobility required to accommodate the changing occupational distribution is referred as structural mobility and in general it is measured by the *index of dissimilarity.* In other words index of dissimilarity measures the amount of mobility introduced by so called structural changes that is, the shifts in occupational distribution. The difference between the total volume of mobility and the minimum structural mobility has often been denoted *Exchange mobility.* It reflects the turnover or exchange among individuals and positions rather than formation of new positions. The index dissimilarity is computed as follows:

Index of dissimilarity = Ä=1/2 ε t [at—bt] In the present study occupational mobility of Yerukulas is analysed through Inter-generational occupational mobility and as well as Intra-generational occupational.

Inter-generational Occupational Mobility : Occupational adherence and change spanning four generations were analysed to examine the inter-generational occupational mobility trends and there by to assess the impact of development programmes, social exclusion, inclusion and equality of life chances. The four generations are respondent Grand father (G_1) respondent father (G_2) respondent (G_3)

and respondent adult employed sons (G_4). The G_1 generation correspondence to the time period 1930 and above; G_2 generation correspondence to the time period 1950 and above; G_3 generation correspondence to the time period 1970 onwards; and G_4 generation correspondence time period 1990 onwards.

The G_1 generation represents pre-independence (British India) period. During this period the Yerukulas were haunted by criminal tribe's act 1871 and were under constant police surveillance and were highly stigmatised. Though, the Yerukula were trying to settle down to lead sedentary life, they were not allowed by many villages. Because of stigma of criminal tribes they were also not increased to participate in agrarian's activities, the prime source of livelihood during that period. Further most rural occupations including the artisan activities were caste based and monopolised by specific castes which specialised artisan activities by tradition. Thus, Yerukula were and provides their some food security left with very much restricted livelihood opportunities. Therefore a large number of them have taken to pig-rearing. Herding pigs involves movement from one village to other (occupationally marginalised and socially excluded and were). Thus the nomadic nature of the Yerukulas persisted in G_1 generation. By rearing pigs they cloud move to the villages, the use of pig dung as organic manure by the farmers as slowly led to a harmonious relationship between the villagers and the Yerukulas. This has helped to ease the antagonistic attitude towards Yerukulas as the members of criminal tribes. Further interaction with the agrarian communities facilitated the search for indigenous alternative livelihood opportunities. In this search, Yerukula found spilt bamboo basket weaving as one of the livelihood source. Split bamboo basket weaving incidentally is one of the occupational affiliations for Madera Caste. The rise in agrarian activities and market activities has given a fillip for the demand to bamboo baskets and allowed bamboo products.

The second generation G_2 represents early decades of India's independence. This period witnessed several for reaching structural changes. Which include legislation and progressives social emancipation and welfare of the down-trodden; socio-economic reforms development of infrastructural inputs universal adult franchise etc., the criminal tribe act was repealed in the period of G_2 generation.

This prompted Yerukulas to lead a more sedentary life. The various programmes of land reforms enabled some of these members to acquire marginal land holdings. The accelerated agrarian, industrial and construction activities created good demand for bamboo baskets. Thus, split bamboo weaving could become a stable source of livelihood. Further, the report built by previous generations, shunning of criminal activities and the skill in basket weaving have prompted the villagers to tolerate the Yerukula settlements and habitats. Thus, relatively speaking Yerukulas were more acceptable. Yet, they were not liberally accepted in the use and participation of public institutions like educational institutions. The only exceptions were those promoted by committed social welfare organisations sponsored by government or by certain other religious institutions like Christian missionaries.

G_3 generation represents a period of poverty alleviation programmes, spread of public distribution system, Banks Nationalisation, distribution of surplus land to weaker sections, stress on amelioration of poor living condition of the weaker sections, encouragement to the health and literacy promotion programmes. During this period G_3 generation began to experience the fruits of development inputs sown in the first three decades of the Independence. The most fore was the decline of stigma if not total elimination of the social stigma. They are now relatively free to choose occupations of their choice. They were also accepted to pursue livelihood pursuits related to agriculture including vending, trading, agriculture commodities, and some of them could gain certain of education and forward skills, healthcare and schooling for children.

The G_4 generation represents a period of globalisation. During this period a grater accent and emphasis on universalisation of primary education, mother and child health, poverty reduction programmes etc were laid. This period represents a period of hope and achievement. The social restrictions and taboos have become much more liberal and flexible. At least in the arena of public interaction and participation.

The broad occupational distribution during the four generations of Yerukulas under reference is presented in table 4.3 our data shows that all the Yerukulas during G_1 and G_2 generations were involved in traditional occupations only. The pursuit of traditional occupations started declining from G_3 generation. 42 per cent of Yerukulas in G_3 generation were involved in non-traditional occupational pursuits. In other words, 58 per cent of the members were found to be adhering to traditional occupational pursuits. Further decline in the involvement of traditional occupations is observed during G_4 generation. Our data revels that only 21.5 per cent of G_4 generation members were involved in traditional occupational pursuits.

Table 4.3. Occupational Distribution of Yerukulas Four Generations

	G1	G2	G3	G4
Modern	-	-	31 10.3%	53 51.9%
Cultivation	-	-	27 9%	18 17.6%
Business	-	-	25 8.3%	5 4.9%
Traditional	300	300	174 58%	22 21.5%
Agriculture labour	-	-	43 14.3%	4 3.9%
Total	**300**	**300**	**300**	**102**

The non-traditional occupations represent agriculture labour, cultivation Business (trading, vending etc) and modern occupations. Thus our data suggests that the occupational involvement and occupational opportunity structure has opened up during the G_3 generation and has considerably, widened during the G_4 generations. In other words the impact of developmental programmes has begun and felt during the G_3 generation 10.3 percent of G_3 generations members were found to be involved in modern occupations; and this has increased to 51.9 percent among the G_4 generation members. Similarly, 9 percent of the G_3 generation members were found to be involved in the pursuit of the cultivation; where as it has increased to 17.6 percent among the G_4 generation members. The occupational distribution by category across the four generations in presented in table 4.3.

Table 4.4. Category wise Occupational Distributions

	G_1	G_2	G_3	G_4
Professional	-	-	4 1.3%	20 19.6%
Executive	-	-	-	10 9.8%
White collar	-	-	2 0.6%	10 9.8%
Skilled	-	-	1 0.3%	5 4.9%
Business	-	-	25 8.3%	5 4.9%
Semi- Skilled	-	-	24 8.0%	8 7.8%
Cultivation	-	-	27 9.0%	18 17.6%
Agriculture Labour	-	-	43 14.3%	4 3.9%
Traditional	300	300	174 58.0%	22 21.5%
Others	-	-	-	-
Total	300	300	300	102

Our data (table 4.4) reveals that unlike in the previous generation, G_4 generation members represent all occupational categories.

This trend indicates not only beginning of social inclusion but also the increasing trend of better life chances for Yerukulas.

However, it must be pointed out here that the educational attainments are very low and as such the level of modern occupations (Profession, Executive, White collar, Skilled occupations) are of lower cadres. For instance, the profession represents only school teachers but not medical doctors, scientists, engineers or professor; executive positions represent only police constables but not higher level executives; skilled occupations represent only drivers but technicians.

On the other hand it must be recognised and stressed that these are achieved positions; and are of secular in native; and a beginning has been made in countering the social stigma. Further, the dependence on traditional occupations has very much declined.

The comparison of G_2 and G_3 generation is analysed in table 4.5 *(See Table on page 130)*. As mentioned earlier all the members of G_2 generation were involved in traditional occupations like basket weaving, pig-raring, trading cattle etc.

However, during the G_3 generation due to the overall development and the resultant change only 58 per cent have adhered to parent conferred ascriptive occupations. 42 per cent have moved into non-traditional occupations. Only 14.3 per cent were involved in manual pursuits like agriculture labour, construction labour.

Thus our analysis shows that 42 per cent of G_3 generations (Respondent) were occupationally mobile. The minimum structural mobility occurred during this period was

41.9 per cent and the exchange mobility was 0.1 per cent In other words, the occupational structure was opening up for Yerukulas but there were not enough number of qualified/ confident people to move in to these newly created opportunity for want of educational attainment and formal training.

The inter-generational occupational mobility between G_3 and G_4 generation was analysed and presented are table 4.6. Our analysis reveals that 81.3 per cent of G_4 generation members were occupationally mobile. In other words only 18.6 per cent have followed the parent conferred ascription livelihood pursuits. Only 11.7 percent experienced downward mobility. That is they were involved in such pursuits which were lower in rank to their parents. 69.7 per cent of the G_4 members have experienced upward mobility. In other words they have moved into such occupations which of an higher rank than their parents. 39.2 per cent were involved in profession, Executive, White collar positions like Teacher, Police Constable, Clerk, Conductors etc. But as mentioned earlier these are of low rank positions, through it was considerably high rank in a relative comparison to their parents occupational positions.

The minimum structural mobility experienced during this period was 53.96 per cent and the exchange mobility was 27.34 per cent. This indicators broader occupational/livelihood opportunities.

Thus, our analysis shows that as a result of the impact of development programmes considerable changes have taken place in the occupational opportunity structure. The changes in the occupational structure have opened-up new occupations and livelihood pursuits, for the benefit of Yerukula members. These changes are more conspicuous during the G_4 generation. The comparison of inheritance and non-inheritance and inter-generational occupational mobility is analysed and presented in tables 4.5 and 4.6.

Table 4.5. Inter-generational Occupational Mobility (G_3)

G_2		I	II	III	IV	V	VI	VII	VIII	IX	X	Total
Professional	I	-	-	-	-	-	-	-	-	-	-	-
Executive	II	-	-	-	-	-	-	-	-	-	-	-
White collar	III	-	-	-	-	-	-	-	-	-	-	-
Skilled	IV	-	-	-	-	-	-	-	-	-	-	-
Business	V	-	-	-	-	-	-	-	-	-	-	-
Semi-skilled	VI	-	-	-	-	-	-	-	-	-	-	-
Cultivation	VII	-	-	-	-	-	-	-	-	-	-	-
Agriculture Labour	VIII	-	-	-	-	-	-	-	-	-	-	-
Traditional	IX	4	-	2	1	25	24	27	43	174	-	300
Others	X	-	-	-	-	-	-	-	-	-	-	-
Total		**4**	**-**	**2**	**1**	**25**	**24**	**27**	**43**	**174**	**-**	**300**

Mobile (126) = 42%

Percentage of Immobile (174) = 58%

Minimum Structural Mobility = 41.9(½ $\xi t_1 - t_2$ absolute)

Exchange Mobility = 0.1

Table 4.6. (G_4) Inter-generational Occupational Mobility (G_4)

G_3		I	II	III	IV	V	VI	VII	VIII	IX	X	Total
Professional	I	-	1	-	-	-	-	-	-	-	-	1
Executive	II	-	-	-	-	-	-	-	-	-	-	-
White collar	III	3	-	-	-	-	-	-	-	-	-	3
Skilled	IV	-	-	-	-	-	-	-	-	-	-	-
Business	V	-	-	1	-	-	-	1	-	-	-	2
Semi-skilled	VI	-	-	-	1	-	-	1	-	-	-	2
Cultivation	VII	2	2	2	-	-	1	6	-	-	-	13
Agriculture Labour	VIII	1	-	-	-	3	1	3	-	9	-	17
Traditional	IX	14	7	7	4	2	6	7	4	13	-	64
Others	X	-	-	-	-	-	-	-	-	-	-	-
Total		**20**	**10**	**10**	**5**	**5**	**8**	**18**	**4**	**22**	**-**	**102**

Mobile (83) = 81.3%

Percentage of Immobile (19) = 18.6%

Minimum Structural Mobility = 53.96 (½ $\epsilon t_1 - t_2$ absolute)

Exchange Mobility = 27.34

Intra-generational Occupational Mobility

The analysis is carried out, by adopting *intra-generational occupational mobility approach by using mobility matrix.* For this purpose the respondent's first adult occupational pursuit at the age of 20 years and the occupational pursuit at the time of data collection were considered. Majority of Yerukulas were found to be involved in more than one occupational pursuit and hence primary occupation as reported by the respondents alone have been considered for the purpose of analysis.

The occupational distribution of respondents at two time intervals *viz*: respondent's first adult occupation at the age of 20 years ($t_{1).}$ And the respondent's primary occupation (t_2) now (in the year 2006) is presented in the mobility matrix.

In the mobility matrix the occupational distribution of the two time intervals are arranged exactly in rows (t_1) and column (t_2) to match and to observe the occupational shifts (mobility). The corresponding diagonal cells of the rows and columns denote the distribution of occupational immobility.

The mobility analysis shows that a large percentage of respondents (58.0) per cent) are involved in traditional occupation. However, of the 174 respondents involved in traditional occupation for 41 respondents it was not parent conferred. It is interesting to note that 84 respondents have deviated from their parent conferred traditional first adult occupations. They have moved into better occupations ranging from semi-skilled to professional pursuits. Similarly, Yerukulas also have deviated from the pursuits of cultivation to other jobs and some of them even reverted to their traditional pursuits.

Thus, our analysis reveals that Yerukulas do not meekly bow down to tradition/parent conferred positions. Instead they constantly strive to improve their positions and aspire to acquire new skills if an opportunity is provided.

Our mobility analysis thus reveals that a good percentage of Yerukulas are mobile (51.0); the mobility is mostly from traditional and cultivation occupations; of which 32.0 per cent are upwardly mobile and only 19.0 per cent are downwardly mobile; these were those who reverted from Semi-skilled and cultivation pursuits.

The index of dissimilarly measure reveals that the minimum structural mobility occurred during the two time intervals was 29.35 per cent. But the percentage of mobile Yerukula respondents were 51.0 per cent and thus the exchange mobility was 21.65 per cent. In other words there were not enough qualified mobile Yerukula respondents to move into the positions/opportunities that have resulted on account of structural shifts of the occupational distribution. *(Table 4.7 and 4.8)*

Table 4.7. Intra-generational Occupational Mobility
Present occupation

Yerukula Respondents previous 20 years		I	II	III	IV	V	VI	VII	VIII	IX	X	Total
Professional	I	-	-	-	-	-	1	-	-	-	-	1
Executive	II	-	-	-	-	-	-	-	-	-	-	-
White collar	III	-	-	-	-	-	-	-	-	-	-	-
Skilled	IV	-	-	-	-	-	-	-	-	-	-	-
Business	V	-	-	-	-	-	-	-	-	-	-	-
Semi-skilled	VI	-	-	-	-	1	5	1	5	-	-	12
Cultivation	VII	1	-	-	1	6	2	7	9	31	-	57
Agriculture Labour	VIII	-	-	-	-	-	1	-	2	10	-	13
Traditional	IX	3	-	2	-	18	15	19	27	133	-	217
Others	X	-	-	-	-	-	-	-	-	-	-	-
Total		4	-	2	1	25	24	27	43	174	-	300

Index of Disseminate = ½ ξ (Absolute) = ½ € (58.7)
= ½ (10) = 5 = ½ × 58.7
= 29.35

Percentage of Immobile (147) = 49.00
Mobile (153) = 51.00
Minimum Structural Mobility (1d) = 29.35
Exchange Mobility = 21.65
% of Upward Mobile = 32.00
Downward Mobile = 19.00

Table 4.8. Intra-generational Occupational Mobility

	t_1Previous Occupation	(%)	t_2Present Occupation	(%)
Professional	1	0.3	4	1.3
Executive	0	-	0	-
White collar	0	-	2	0.6
Skilled	0	-	1	0.3
Business	0	-	25	8.3
Semi-skilled	12	4.0	24	8.0
Cultivation	57	19.0	27	9.0
Agriculture Labour	13	4.3	43	14.3
Traditional	217	72.5	174	58.0

Upward

Percentage of Mobile	=	32.00
Downward Mobile	=	19.00
Mobile	=	51.00
Immobile	=	49.00
Minimum Structural Mobility	=	29.35
Exchange Mobility	=	21.65

As our data suggest this is primarily due to lack of needed skills and educational attainments on part of the Yerukulas and thus, they are deprived of equality of opportunity as envisaged by the constitution of India.

Trends of Occupational Mobility

The amount of occupational mobility due to splits in occupational distributions introduced by structural changes during the four generations under reference is measured by the index of dissimilarity and is deniable by minimum structural mobility (MSM). The turn over away individuals and occupational positions is denied by exchange mobility. The findings of the analysis is presented in table 4.9.

Table 4.9. Trends of occupational mobility

	G_1	G_2	G_2	G_3	G_3	G_4
Mobile	Nil	Nil	Nil	42.0%	39.6%	81.3%
M.S.M	Nil	Nil	Nil	41.9%	41.1%	53.96%
Exchange	Nil	Nil	Nil	0.1%	1.4%	27.34%

Our analysis reveals that during the G_1 and G_2 generations no occupational shifts took place due to structural changes and as such there was no mobility. This period refers to British India and very early decades of Independence.

However, after Independence several developmental programmes were launched through the five-year plans. These have unheard structural changes and resulted in occupational shifts. The structural changes and the consequent occupational shifts have increased as the decades and five-year plans progressed. The G_3 and G_4 generations fall under period and have experienced occupational mobility.

The Inter-generational trends show that the period between G_2 and G_3 the structural mobility occurred was 41.9 per cent. In other words during this period shifts in occupational distribution due to structural changes took place. Though 42 per cent of G_3 members were mobile, they could not make use of these shift, as most of them were not suited to the newly created opportunities. Hence the exchange mobility was only 0.1 per cent.

The Intra-generational occupational mobility analyse through light on the occupational mobility that, occurred during the G_3 generation period. The G_3 generation which corresponds to the period of 1970 and above stated experience the fruitful and beneficial impact of the developmental programmes that were lunched since 1950 (independence). As a result the 39.6 percent of G_3 members were mobile and the minimum structural mobility introduced was 41.1 percent. But as most of the G_3 members were not qualified in terms of requisites skills and educational attainment they could not benefit from these opportunities and thus exchange mobility was only 1.4 per cent. The mobility experienced by these members was revolved around cultivation, business, semi-skilled and manual occupations.

The structural changes have introduced greater occupational shifts during the G_3 and G_4 generations (1990 onwards) and as a result the minimum structural mobility occurred was 53.96 per cent during G_4 generations. 81.3 per cent of the G_4 members were occupationally mobile. Some of the G_4 unlike their parents could attain through of low levels, modern education and skills. Therefore an exchange mobility requisite was 27.34 per cent.

Thus, our analysis shows that there is progressive increase in mobility trends among Yerukulas over the generations. There is increasing trend of deviation from parent conferred traditional occupations and inclusive into the emerging modern occupational structure. But in terms of equality of opportunity the Yerukulas are still left behind (social excluded) due to want of better levels of educational and skills attainments and they could not avail the opportunities that are emerging due to structural changes and the resulted occupational shifts.

SECTION—II

Access to Education

Education is intrinsic to human personality. It carries both intrinsic as well as instrumental values. Education is enlightenment and enlightenment is empowerment'. Education is an empowering force that endows its recipient with such qualities of the head, the heart and the hand and liberates him from all imaginable human infirmities and elevates him form all disabilities. (*Atkinson, A.B.* 1998)

Thus Education is a cornerstone of empowerment of human society because it creates capacity to respond to opportunities, to challenge their traditional roles and to change their lives. Hence, Education is a source of power and also is an agency that empowers people. Education is a powerful tool for empowerment of individual.

Historically, unequal access to education has been rampant in India. Discriminatory order in the caste system has been instrumental for this. Because in ancient times, there was a distinctive spiritual meaning associated with education (*A.Pathak,* 2002) and meant the realisation of the ultimate and the absolute and the overcoming of all earthly temptations and desires.

In the current scenario, the educational goals have become secular and are primarily the acquisition of technical skills needed to achieve excellence in the techno-economic world. Babasaheb Ambedkar observed that education is the right weapon to cut the social slavery and to enlighten the downtrodden masses to come up and gain social status, economic betterment and political freedom. Education thus is chosen to be the prime instrument for transforming India from a poor depending technologically backward country into an advanced nation. Further it is viewed that massification of education, including higher education is the likely key to massification of human welfare. (*Cantillon*, E.2002)

Broad-based efforts made during the last fifty years have resulted in a massive expansion of the education system in the country, raising the overall status of educational provisions in terms of accessibility and participation. The expansion of the education system in the country has also expanded tremendously at all levels such as school education, higher education, technical education, adult education, etc.

Education of SCs and STs is improving gradually due to the efforts of thee government especially plan expenditure on different sectors. When we look at the all-India picture the plan expenditure on elementary education of SCs and STs has risen from 58 per cent to 65.6 per cent during 1951-56 to 2002-07 (the tenth plan period). Similarly, the plan expenditure on secondary education has also increased from 5 per cent to 9.9 per cent during the period under consideration. Further, the plan expenditure on higher education rose from 8 per cent to 9.5 per cent whereas technical education declined form 14 per cent to 10.7 per cent. Again the plan expenditure on adult education increased from 2 per cent to 2.9 per cent.

Yet, the irony is that Education is a privilege rather than a right for the children of India. Many children can only attend school when they are not working. Despite efforts at social and economic development since attainment of independence, a majority of our people continue to remain deprived of education. The disadvantaged groups have not realised the importance of using education as a transformative project due to several social rigidities.

Social exclusion is also considered in a particular way. As a fact of life, we know that the same group of people who participate in some social relations may, at the same time, be excluded from others. Hence, to say that a person is excluded from something is a purely descriptive statement, with no analytical value. In analytical terms, the question is whether there is *some exclusion* that has important effects upon social inequality. Which are these exclusions in a particular society? Social exclusion manifests itself in the lack of an individual's access to functioning's as compared to other members of society. Under the heading of social exclusion are included concerns for social phenomena as diverse as poverty, low educational attainment, unemployment and other labour market disadvantages, poor housing and lack of access to social and political institutions. Broadly speaking, a person is said to be socially excluded if it is unable to participate in the basic economic and social activities of the society it lives in. (*Atkinson, Cantillon, Marlier and Nolan* (2002).)

Yerukulas and Access to Education

In the light of the above and therefore, in the present section access to education is examined in a longitudinal manners.

In other words, access to education is examined were a period of four generations of Yerukulas under reference. Such as examination will through light not only are the impact of developmental programmes that also as in social exclusion and inclusion of Yerukulas and their social transformation.

The total population of the three hundred Yerukula households under reference is found to be 1415 members, of these respondents (G_3) constitute 21.25 per cent, respondents wives constitute 18.9 per cent, respondents sons constitute 27.76 per cent, daughters constitute 18.63 per cent, Grandsons and Granddaughters constitute 5.85 and 3.18 per cent respectively; daughter-in-laws 4.8 per cent (*See Table 4.10 on next page*).

The average age of the respondents is found to be 45.06 years and that their wives is found to be 33.2 years. The average age of the respondent's sons is found to be 13.5 years. However, 79 sons out of a total 392 sons were found to be above the age group 16 years; the average age of the daughters is reportedly 9.4 years. The average age of grand son and granddaughter is 9.2 and 8.5 years respectively; and that of daughter-in-laws is found to be 22.67 years; 11.1 per cent of the family members under reference are below the age of five years. 39 per cent are in the school going age group of 6 to 15 years. 44.04 per cent are in the age group of 16 to 50 years.

The workers constitute 49.59 per cent. Child workers among the total 558, working members of Yerukula families were found to be the child workers below the age of 10 years; and 22.9 per cent were found to be child workers in the age group of 11 to 15 years. Thus, our study reveals that child labour is rampant among the Yerukula families; in other words 30 per cent of children of the Yerukula families are denied and deprived of schooling opportunities and thus are socially excluded. The deprivation is partly due to their poverty-stricken loving conditions, nomadic way of life but not due to social stigma. (*See Table 4.11 on page 140*)

Table 4.10. Respondent and Family Members and Age Differentials

	0-5	6-10	11-15	16-20	21-30	31-40	41-50	51 above	Total	Avr. Age	%
Respondent (G)	-	-	-	-	31	63	133	73	300	45.06	21.25
Wife(G_3)	-	-	-	1	29	150	72	15	267	33.2	18.9
Sons(G_4)	43	136	134	24	49	6	-	-	392	13.5 12.33%	27.76
Daughters(G_4)	25	171	65	2	-	-	-	-	263	9.4 8.78%	18.63
Grandsons(G_5)	54	24	4	-	1	-	-	-	83	9.2 4.8%	5.87
Granddaughters(G_5)	35	9	1	-	-	-	-	-	45	8.5 3.8%	3.18
Daughter-in-laws	-	-	-	26	35	1	-	-	62	22.67	4.8
Total	**157** **11.1%**	**340** **24.07%**	**204** **14.4%**	**53** **3.7%**	**145** **10.26%**	**220** **15.58%**	**205** **14.5%**	**88** **6.2%**	**1412**	-	-

Table 4.11. Respondent's Family members age and work participation

Age	Worker	Non-worker	Total	Percentage
0- 5	-	157	157	14.05
6-10	43 7.7% 12.60%	297 87.35% 87.35%	340(100)	30.43
11-15	128 22.9% 52.74%	76 37.25%	204	18.26
16-50	384 68.8% 96.96%	12	396	35.45
51 above	3 0.5%	17	20	1.79
Total	**558** **49.95%**	**559** **50.05%**	**1117**	-
Average age		26.6	11.70 9.1%	20.36 17.85%

Educational attainments

The educational attainment of respondents and their family members is presented in table 4.12. Our study reveals that 52.2 per cent of the Yerukula members are illiterate. 11.07 per cent of the members were found to be children below the age of six years. Less than one per cent has studied above the secondary level; only 3.11 per cent have received education up to secondary level; 5.85 per cent have studied up to upper primary; 26.67 per cent have studied up to primary level.

76.33 per cent of respondents are illiterates. Illiteracy is rather very high among the Yerukula women. 95.5 per cent of respondents wives were illiterates; and 40 per cent of daughters were also illiterate. Only two respondents (0.6%), received collegiate education. 4.3 per cent of the respondents

Table 4.12. Respondent's Family members of Education Levels

	Illiterate	Literate	Primary	Upper -primary	Secondary	10+2	College	N.A	Total
Respondent	229	-	35	21	10	3	2	-	300
Wife	255	1	8	1	1	-	1	-	267
Son	99	-	175	39	29	4	3	43	392
Daughter	93	-	120	20	4	1	-	25	263
Grandson	2	-	26	1	-	-	-	54	83
Granddaughter	-	-	9	1	-	-	-	35	45
Daughter-in-law	57	-	5	-	-	-	-	-	62
Father	1	-	-	-	-	-	-	-	1
Mother	4	-	-	-	-	-	-	-	4
Total	**740**	**1**	**378**	**82**	**44**	**8**	**6**	**157**	**1417**
	52.22%		**26.67%**	**5.85%**	**3.11%**	**0.4%**	**0.4%**	**11.07%**	

only have completed secondary education. On the contrary 71.63 per cent of respondent's sons are literate among them nine per cent have completed secondary level of education and three members received collegiate education.

Access to Education Inter-generational Trends

The Inter-generational trends of educational attainments reveals a progressive inclusiveness. During the grand father (G_1) generation all the members were illiterate. This was because of their social exclusion on account social stigma as criminal tribes and also due to their nomadic life. They represent the time period between 1930-1950.

Among the fathers generation (G_2) 99 per cent were illiterates. Though the severity of social exclusion was relatively less, the opportunities for schooling and the needed social encouragement were near total absent. They represent the time period between 1950 and above.

During respondents generation (G_3) 76.33 per cent were illiterate. Social exclusion on account of social stigma has considerably reduced. The Government sponsored schooling opportunities were available in selected villages. The respondents whose families enjoyed relatively stable livelihood could avail these opportunities. Further, the respondent's generation's childhood corresponds to the period around the decade 1970's. By this time the opportunities for schooling were fairly well developed. The severity of social exclusion on account of social stigma too has declined. This was mostly due to the settled and sedentary life style of Yerukulas and their occupational pursuits such as basket weaving, agriculture and pig-rearing. This is not to say that the social stigma of criminality has disappeared. Time to time police check-ups continued and Tribes criminal tendencies were still fresh in the minds of general populace. The overall developments such as communications urbanisation, public facilities like school, hospital and such developmental programmes as employment programme, rural development programmes literacy promotes had a bearing on the changes in life style of Yerukulas.

The illiteracy percentage has vastly come down to 28.37 per cent during the respondent's son generation (G_4). The G_4 and G_5 generation by and large corresponds to the post 1990's period. By this period rapid strides of developments have taken place in the state. Most important is special emphasis on universalisation of primary education. Special mission mode activity was undertaken to reach the unreached for enrolment. Further the living conditions have improved. Relatively better stability of livelihood was attained. Food security though foodgrain supply by Public Distribution System for subsidised price, Mid-day meals programmes, free schooling were launched and well under way. Social stigma is considerably weakened and this has further reduced to a rare 6.89 percent during respondents grandsons generation (G_5) (*See Table 4.13 on next page*).

Thus our analysis reveals that during the Pre-Independence and the early decades of Independence period the Yerukulas experienced total social exclusion with reference to educational opportunities. During the Post-independent era however, Yerukulas have been experiencing though slow but study inclusiveness with regards to educational opportunities and this is particularly during the very recent decades.

However, it may be pointed out here that in terms of levels of educational attainments the Yerukulas still experience social exclusion. This is evident from the fact that less than one per cent of Yerukulas under reference have received collegiate level of education. Further, the level of literacy attainments among the Yerukula women is very poor. In other words, the impact of Tribal Development Programmes for the promotion of literacy was not very successful at least with regards to Yerukula. However, the effort of Sarva Siksha Abiyan for univerlisation of primary education has been successful enough to reach more than 70 per cent of Yerukula children.

Thus our analysis reveals the following broad trends in relation to access to educational opportunities.

Table 4.13. Educational Attainments—Inter-generational Trends

Levels of Education	Grand Father (G_1)	Father (G_2)	Respondent (G_3)	Son (G_4) N=349	Grand Son (G_5)N=29	Wife(G_3)	Daughter (G_4)N=238	Grand daughter (G_5)N=10
Illiterate	300 (100%)	297 99%	229 76.33%	99 28.37%	2 6.89%	255 95.5%	93 39.08%	Nil
Literate	Nil	3 1.0%	-	-	-	1 0.3%	-	-
Primary	Nil	Nil	35 11.6%	175 50.14%	26	8 2.9%	120 50.42%	9
Upper - Primary	Nil	Nil	21 7.0%	39 11.17%	1	1 0.3%	20 8.4%	1
Secondary	Nil	Nil	10 3.3%	29 8.3%	-	1 0.3%	4 1.6%	Nil
10+2	Nil	Nil	3 1.0%	4 1.1%	-	Nil	1 0.42%	Nil
College	Nil	Nil	2 0.6%	3 0.8%	-	1 0.3%	-	Nil
N.A	Nil	Nil	-	43 12.3%	54	-	25 10.5%	35
Total	**300**	**300**	**300**	**392**	**83**	**267**	**263**	**45**

As far as access to literacy, the stigmatised tribe of Yerukula is experiencing slow social inclusiveness. But to attain even this, they took five generations of time. Yet, they experiences and there persists social exclusions in terms of gender discrimination, as the female literacy levels are very poor among the Yerukula. Second, the levels of educational attainments is very low, it is only up to primary or upper primary level, and less than one percent of the Yerukulas under reference have received collegiate level of education. Thirdly, child labour persists among Yerukulas; 30 per cent of Yerukula children were involved as child workers and thus they are deprived, denied schooling opportunities and experience social exclusion. It was observed that even the children in the tender age group of 6 to 10 years are involved as child workers. Their involvement in child work is as pig rearing and begging and other menial and miscellaneous activities. These trends point out the need for focused attention on Yerukulas by the Tribal Development Agencies. Tribal Development in Plain areas generally availed by other numerically dominant tribal groups such as Sugalies.

Further, the semi-nomadic nature of Yerukulas is another contributory factor and this is heighted by numerically very small size of Yerukula population spread in any given habitation and lack of local identity as tribal Thanda.

SECTION—III

Access to Healthcare

Prior to Independence access to healthcare promotions were not only poor but also scarce. Particularly in the rural areas. The healthcare delivery was to within the framework of caste structure and many of sections were depend of and socially excluded from the healthcare. As such these sections have deprived their own indigenous.

The C.D.P launched that Independence, that

Independence, about reasonable new work of modern health care institutes and services which are scheme in their service.

The status of access to healthcare can be understand in terms of access to reproductive healthcare practias.

Access to Reproductive Healthcare is examined with reference to

- Place of birth
- Delivery attendance
- Immunisation
- ANC/ANA/PNC
- Mortality
- Infant feeding
- Trends

Reproductive Health Practices

Place of Birth Delivery Practices: The incidence of maternal mortality from sepsis and neonatal tetanus is attributed largely to the lack of simple hygienic practices such as clean hands clean perineum and clean cord. In India, particularly rural India, birth deliveries are conducted under unhygienic conditions (*Kumar et al,* 1988; *Sharma and Bali,* 1989) one of the important thrusts of the reproductive and child healthcare is to encourage deliveries under proper hygienic conditions and under the supervision of skilled health professionals.

Birth deliveries during the Grandfather (G_1) and Father (G_2) periods were home deliveries only. This practice continued to greater extent even during respondent's period. Majority of the Birth Deliveries during respondent's period were Home Deliveries (79 per cent). But in the recent time that is sons generation this practice has shifted to institutional deliveries. All the birth deliveries were institutional deliveries. In other words the young Yerukula women have access to institutional services. (Table 4.14)

Table 4.14. Birth of Delivery

	G_1	G_2	G_3	G_4
Home	300	300	196 65.3%	-
Intuitional (Hospital)	-	-	104 34.6%	269
Total	**300**	**300**	**300**	**269**

Delivery Attendance: The proportion of births delivered by untrained attendants is gradually decreasing from the year 1971. Even so, there are rural areas of the country where nine out of ten births are delivered by an untrained attendant (*Khan et al,* 1986; *Kantikar* and *Sinha*, 1989)

During the G_1 period all the birth deliveries were attended by the untrained elderly women of the community. This trend evidences the *social exclusiveness* of that period. This social exclusiveness continued even during the G_2 period. In other words the social stigma of criminal tribe made them as social exclusives. Thus Yerukulas were deprived of even traditional and semi-professional medical care.

But this trend has changed during G_3 and G_4 generations for different reasons. The Criminal Tribe Act was repealed by the year 1952. The respondents unlike their fathers now no longer nomadic and is leading sedentary settled life and acceptable pursuits and has developed symbiotic relationship with other communities. In addition community development programmes particularly healthcare programmes were relatively more accessible.

The Birth delivery during respondent period (G_3) was mostly attendant by the untrained traditional local midwife (63.6 per cent), who generally was a non-Yerukula woman. 34.7 per cent were attended by trained nurses and qualified doctors. But in the case of son's generation (G_4) they were attended by trained nurses (56.8 per cent) and by doctors 43.12 per cent irrespective of rural and urban divide. This indicates access and reach to professional and modern health care. (Table 4.15)

Table 4.15. Delivery Attendance

	G_1	G_2	G_3	G_4
Untrained Elderly women	300	291 97.0%	5 1.6%	-
Traditional Midwife (Manthrasani)		9 3.0%	191 64.7%	-
Trained dai	-	-	-	-
ANM/Nurse	-	-	82 27.7%	153 56.8%
Doctor	-	-	22 7.4%	116 43.12%
Total	**300**	**300**	**295**	**269**

Reproductive Health Services

Immunisation of Expectant Mother: The expectant mothers were required to be immunised against the occurrence of Tetanus to prevent maternal mortality. As a result of poor antenatal immunisation, neonatal tetanus persists. Tetanus is held responsible for anywhere between one and two thirds of all neonatal deaths (*Sokhey*, 1988; *Singh and Paul*, 1988; *Kapil*, 1980; *Agarwal and Agarwal*, 1987; *UNICEF*, 1984). Understandably such services were non-existent during the G_1 period and were rare during the period of G_2. Only 44.33 per cent of mothers during respondents (G_3) period were immunised whereas 85.87 per cent of Yerukulas young women (G_4) received Tetanus Toxoid injection during the pregnancy (Table 4.16)

Table 4.16. Immunisation (Tetanus Toxoid)

	G_1	G_2	G_3	G_4
No	34	32	-	-
No. Response	266	254	-	-
Yes	-	-	133 44.33%	231 85.87%
Total	**300**	**286**	**133**	**231**

Ante-natal Care: A pregnant woman needs six times more iron than non-pregnant women. Iron deficiency leads to anaemia and results in severe complications.

In India a wide range of cultural practices exist regarding diet during pregnancy both on how much to eat and on what to eat. Khan et al, (1988) in their village level study in U.P observed athat even when women are aware of the importance of diet during pregnancy, cultural and economic priorities days them access to better nutrition. As a result, anaemia is widespread among pregnancy women (haemoglobin levels below 11 grams/dl). The spread of anaemia was estimated to range for 40-50 per cent in urban areas and in rural areas 50-70 per cent, (*UNECEF* 1991; *Kaoal* 1990; *Bhardwaj* 1990; *Mathai* 1989).

Anaemia is a leading direct cause of maternal deaths. It also contributes indirectly by aggravating other complications of pregnancy such as eclampria; antepartues haemorrhage sepsis and genets universal trial, infections. Consequences of material anaemia for infants are equally acute. For example, three fifths of all infants form to women with haemoglobin levels less than 5.0 g/dl was low birth weight, comported to one-quarter of those born to women with normal haemoglobin levels (*Remachandran* 1989).

Prenatal mortality rates are ten times higher among severally anaemic women companied to normal women. Low birth weight infants account far 70 per cent of all prenatal deaths; 90 per cent of all early neonatal deaths; and half of all infant deaths (*Ramaling swami* 1985; *Singh* 1986).

Food and Iron supplementation have been found to impress such material health attributes as weight gain, incidence of anaemia, complications during pregnancy and child birth, and birth weight (*Dava* and *Mitra* 1990, *Iyevar* 1975). The national anaemia prophylaxis programme of Iron and folic acid tables during pregnancy was ante-natal as early as the 1950s. 55.66 per cent of women during G_3 period received IFA supplements. Curiously the young Yerukula women (G_4) have shown scant interest in receiving IFA supplements. Only 13.38 per cent of them received Iron Folic Acid tablets. (Table 4.17)

Table 4.17. Ante-natal Care

	G_1	G_2	G_3	G_4
Iron-Folic Acid tablets	-	-	167 55.66%	36 13.38%
No Response	300	300	-	-
Total	**300**	**300**	**167**	**36**

Ante-natal Advice: The pregnant women need Anti-natal care advice with regard to their diet, danger signal, care etc. As a result of limited ante-natal contests high risk cases escape identification. Risk factors such as age, weight, height, birth interraval, party (one or more than 4, previous height of difficult pregnancy or infants less evidence of ante-natal haemorrhage, poor weight gain (under 5 kg) diarrhoeic, dysentery or fever during pregnancy (*Singh and Paul* 1988). *Kumar and Wadia* 1983 suggest that trained birth attendants do in fact have significantly better healthcare knowledge and can better recognise high-risk conations.

This need was met by such service providing as untrained elderly women of the community during G_1 (100%) and G_2 (95.7%). During the G_3 generation ante-natal advice was provided by such service providers as Mother 4.7 per cent; untrained elderly woman 1.73 per cent; traditional mid-wife (manthrasani) 1.3 per cent; trained health worker 1.3 per cent; ANM/Nurse 83.7 per cent; and doctor 7.3 per cent. During G_4 generation, the younger Yerukula women have received this service from only the skilled health professionals such as ANM/Nurse 43.7 per cent; trained health worker 28.0 per cent; and doctor17.7 per cent. (*See Table 4.18 on next page*)

Post-natal Care/Services: Post-natal care and service during the G_1 and G_2 generations was by the elderly women of the community, (100 per cent and 95.7 per cent respectively). G_3 generation revealed mixed trends. Post-

Table 4.18. Ante-Natal Advice

	G_1	G_2	G_3	G_4
Untrained Elderly women	300	287 95.7%	5 1.7%	-
Mother	-	-	14 4.7%	-
Manthrasani(Traditional Mid wife)	-	1 0.3%	4 1.3%	-
ANM/Nurse	-	12 4.0%	251 83.7%	131
RDT Health worker	-	-	4 1.3%	84
Doctor	-	-	22 7.3%	53
No	-	-	-	1
Total	**300**	**300**	**300**	**269**

natal care and services in the case of respondent wives was by mid-wife (0.3 per cent); followed by mothers (26.3 per cent). The remaining majority were attended by the skilled professional health workers like trained health worker((1.0 per cent); ANM/Nurse (54.7 per cent) and doctor (17.7 per cent).Only in the case of 17.66 per cent doctors services were sought that too in urban and semi-urban areas. Against this scenario in the case of younger Yerukulas women (G_4), the post-natal care and services were offered by doctor (51.7 per cent) followed by ANM/Nurse (32.3 per cent) 0.4 per cent by trained health worker. (*See Table 4.19 on next page*)

Reproductive Health Problems & Mortality

Maternal, Neo-natal and Infant Mortality rates are high in India on account, poor reproductive health practices and care. These are preventable. India is a typical of a high mortality setting. Sepsis, abortions, hemorrhage, toxemia and anemia account for the large majority of all maternal deaths

Table 4.19. Post-Natal Care

	G_1	G_2	G_3	G_4
No	-	-	-	4 1.3%
NA	-	-	-	31 10.3%
Mother	-	2 0.7%	79 26.3%	-
Untrained Elderly Women	300	287 95.7%	-	-
Manthrasani	-	-	1 0.3%	-
ANM/Nurse		11 3.7%	164 54.7%	97 32.3%
RDT Health Worker	-	-	3 1.00%	13 4.3%
Doctor	-	-	53 17.7%	155 51.7%
Total	**300**	**300**	**300**	**300**

over the decade of the 1980s (Registrar General 1987; Bhatia1988). By and large, well over two-thirds of all maternal deaths are held to be preventable (Agarwal et al 1982; Bhasker Rao 1980; Sinha 1986; Panat and Mehendale 1987).

Over one-quarter of all infant deaths in 1986 were attributed to pre-maturity (27 per cent), almost one-tenth to respiratory infection (9 per cent), and 7 per cent to diarrhoea of the new born. Another 8 per cent resulted from other causes including cord infection.

Studies reiterate that pre natal and neo-natal mortality are overwhelmingly due to maternal factors, notably poor nutrition and inadequate ante-and intra-natal care. Various studies report that prematurity and low birth weight are directly responsible for about one-quarter of all infant deaths and are associated factors in about 50 per cent of all neo-natal deaths (*Roy Chodhary* and *Jayaswal* 1989; *Agarwal* and *Agarwal* 1987; *Singh* and *Paul* 1988). Bactetial infection (mostly tetanus) is responsible for about one-tenth of all early infant deaths (*Singh* and *Paul* 1988).

Our data reveals that still births were as high as 31.7 per cent during respondent's ($G_{3)}$ period. This was reduced to only 4.6 per cent during son's generation (G_4) period. Obviously this is due to better ante and post-natal care and services as well as immunisation of expectant mothers and due to institutional deliveries. However, abortions reported were fewer (5.3 per cent) during respondent's period as against 24.7 per cent during son's generation. The other delivery problems too were less during respondent generation (8.7 per cent) as against 12.00 per cent during son's period. These low figures of the respondent period presumably due to under reporting. (Table 4.20)

Table 4.20. Delivery Problem

	G_1	G_2	G_3	G_4
Still Birth	34	74	93	14
	11.3%	24.7%	31.0%	4.7%
Abortion	1	4	16	74
	0.3%	1.3%	5.3%	24.7%
Other Delivery Problems	124	184	26	36
	41.3%	61.3%	8.7%	12.0%
Total	**159**	**262**	**135**	**124**

Mortality Trends: There is appreciable reduction in neo-natal infant and maternal mortality incidents from G_1 generation to G_4 generation. The neo-natal mortality incidents were fewer in G_1 and G_2 generations (13.7 and 25.7 per cent respectively). It was highest in G_3 generation (46.3 per cent) which was brought down to 36.01 per cent in G_4 generation. Similarly infant mortality incidents were reduced from 61 per cent to 31.3 per cent. However, the incidence of maternal mortality was high during G_1 and G_2 generations (55.3 and 29.7 per cent) and this was brought down to 11.3 per cent during G4 generation. In the case of maternal mortality incidents of respondent's maternal mortality in enhanced from 9.7 per cent to 11.3 per cent.

Majority of the respondents (82.7 per cent) have acknowledged that neo-natal and infant mortality and maternal mortality incidents among them were reduced in the last five years irrespective of rural urban divide. The following reasons were attributed for this reduction. Better child healthcare (17.3 per cent); good environment (5.6 per cent); better medical facilities (11.3 per cent); Provision of medical care (18.3 per cent); and timely vaccines (10.3). (Table 4.21)

Table 4.21. Pregnancy and Mortality

	G_1	G_2	G_3	G_4
Maternal Mortality	166 55.3%	88 29.3%	29 9.7%	34 11.3%
Neo-natal Mortality	41 13.7%	77 25.7%	139 46.3%	108 36.01%
Infant Mortality	46 15.3%	162 54.0%	61 39.0%	94 31.3%
Total	**253**		**229**	**236**

Infant Feeding Practices: The practice of breast feeding the infant is rather declining in the case of younger Yerukula women. 47 per cent of young women depend upon other sources such as cow/buffalo milk; milk-powder. (Table 4.22)

Table 4.22. Infant Feeding

	G_1	G_2	G_3	G_4
Mother's Milk	300	300	280 93.3%	128 42.7%
By Cows Milk	-	-	4 1.3%	45 15.0%
Goat/Sheep	-	-	3 1.0%	28 9.3%
Tin Milk	-	-	13 4.3%	68 22.7%
NA	-	-	-	31
Total	**300**	**300**	**300**	**300** **10.3%**

SECTION - IV

Social Stigma: Social Exclusion and Inclusion

In the present section an attempt is made to examine the social exclusion and inclusion of Yerukulas. For this purpose longitudinal study of *changes in the levels of living* among the Yerukula tribe of Rayalaseema in the last ten decades is attempted by comparing four generations of Yerukulas. More specifically our analysis is pertained to the *Assessment* with regard to the *changes in the levels of Standard of living, Quality of life* and *Social well-being* across four generations *i.e.* Grand father (G_1), Father ($G_{2)}$ Respondent (G_3) and Respondent Adult employed sons (G_4).These four generations space the last one hundred years and covers both Pre-Independence and Post-Independence periods to till date.

The change in the levels of living is understood by examining the changes in the levels of standard of living, quality of life and social well-being across four generations. The assessment is carried out by specially constructed indices of standard of living, quality of life and social well-being.

Standard of Living

Standard of living is an economic concept to assess the living conditions. It is a tool to measure human comfort and happiness objectively. Generally speaking it is an ideal to strive for standard of living refers to a decent, proper, healthy and physically responsible life style for families and is about specific goods and services.

The index of standard of living comprises five indicators such indicators as annual income, livelihood, food security, housing and assets. Each indicator is graded into five grades. These are arranged in a graded manner ranging from low to high. Accordingly weighted scores were assigned from one to five. The composite index of standard of living comprises a maximum of score of 25 and a minimum score of 5. The composite index is graded into five levels of living, such as Very Bad, Bad (6-10), Not So Bad (11-15), Good Enough (16-20) and Satisfactory (21-25) levels.

Annual Incomes are graded 0-3000, 3000-6000, 6000-12000, 12000-18000 and Eighteen thousand and above. The Income eighteen thousand above is considered above poverty line and hence assigned a score of five.

Livelihoods are graded on the basis of their stability. The criterion for stability is based on the duration of employment/ availability of livelihood in a year.

The livelihoods are grades as very un-stable; unstable; seasonal; stable; and very stable livelihood. Very un-stable livelihoods include livelihood practices such as thieving, decoit and hunting. Un-stable livelihood practices comprise semi-skilled pursuits like Tractor-driving, auto-ricksha driving and other odd jobs, seasonal livelihoods include agriculture manual labour and construction labour Commission agency, Cultivation Stable livelihood practices include spilt bamboo basket weaving, pig-rearing, moneylending, etc. Very stable occupations are salaried occupations.

Food Security is graded on the basis of consumption and non-consumption of meals. The quality and the quantity of

Table 4.23. Index of Standard of Livi ng

Indices of Standard of living	G_1	G_2	G_3	G_4*
Lively hood	Very unstable 59.0% Stable 41.00%	stable 100.0%	Stable 18.33%	Very stable 18.33% Stable 21.0% Seasonal 41.33%
Food security	Often starved 100.0%	Often starved 37.0% Food was scarce 53.0%	Not Misseo meals 36.7% Meals twice/a day 61.0%	Meals twice/ thrice a day 89.3%
Housing	Shack 90.3%	Hut 80.7%	Hut 56.7% Kutcha 22.3% Pucca 19.0%	Hut 23.4% Kutcha 19.3% Semi-pucca 11.3% Pucca 36.0%
Assets	Pigs/Fowl 100.0%	Pigs/Fowl 98.3%	Pigs and Movable 32.6 Movable + Immovable 34.3% Costly items 13.6% Nil 4.8%	Movable + Immovable 20.3% Costly items 34.00% Nil 5.00%
Items	>3000 73.0% >6000 27.0%	>6000 99.3%	>12000 73.30% >6000 20.0% >3000 4.7%	<18000 19.00% >12000 69.3%

* 10 per cent are not considered as they are very young.

the meals, however, were not considered due to the problems of memory recall and measurement. Hence, food-security is determined on the frequency of meals consumed in a week. Food security is graded as often starved/, hungry in a week; often missed meals; missed some meals or food was scarce in a week; meals one time only; and meals twice/thrice a day.

Often starved/, hungry in a week was assigned lowest score. Consumption of meals twice or thrice a day is assigned highest score of five.

Housing was judged based on the type of Dwelling they lived in. They are graded as shack; hut; kutcha; semi-pucca; and pucca house. Accordingly pucca housing was given highest score of five; shack was given lowest score of one.

Assets are graded based on the possession. Those who did not hay any assets were given lowest score of one; those who possessed one or two milch cattle, fowls, and sheep are pigs, or rare pigs were given a score of two. In addition to the livestock, those possessed bicycle, rickshaw, radio, etc., movable assets were assigned a score of three. In addition to livestock movable assets those who posses immovable assets like farmland, house site are given score of four. Those who own costly items like gold, motorcycle etc in addition to lively stock and movable and immovable assets were given a score of five. The results of the analysis is presented in table 4.23).

Quality of Life

The study of quality of life is an examination of influence upon the goodness and meaning in life as well as people's happiness and well-being.

The concept of quality of life (quality of life) stands for an idea of well being which is wider than and can not be simply measured by, income and natural consumption or the narrow economic nation of standard of living. Quality of Life stands for idea of well-being which stands which acknowledges people wider needs and indicates subjection life satisfaction. (*Josh Wolfe* 2000)

The Index of Quality of Life comprises five indicators. These are levels of literary; health; source of drinking water and cooking fuel and house lighting.

Each indicator consists of five grades. These are arranged in a graded manner ranging from low to high. Accordingly weighted scores were assigned from one to five. The index of quality of life comprises a maximum of score of 25 and a minimum score of 5. The index is graded into five levels of quality of life, such as Very Bad, Bad (6-10), Not so Bad (11-15), Good enough (16-20) and satisfactory (21-25) levels.

The indicator literacy is graded as illiterate; literate; primary; secondary; and above secondary level.

The health indicator is graded as epidemics; deaths exceed births; births exceed deaths; fewer deaths; and fewer births and deaths.

The indicator on drinking water is graded as open well; tank; river; bore pump; and tap water. *The indicator on cooking fuel* is graded as fire wood; kerosene; gas; electricity; and solar energy. *The indicator on house lighting* is grades as oil lamp; kerosene; petromax light; gas light; and electricity. The results of the analysis is presented in table 4.24.

Social Well-being

In a sustainable community, equity, education, respect for human rights and the meeting of basic needs combine to create social wealth. Everyone has the right to access to a safe and healthful environment in which to live, work, play and learn, including contact with nature through access to other species. Everyone has the right to the fulfillment of basic human needs, including safe and healthful shelter, dignified work, sufficient food, education that meets their needs and skills. Everyone has the right to be part of a community that offers mutual respect. (*Jorge Lara-Braud*, 1999).

Social well-being is sometimes described in terms of the three e's, especially among the Sustainable Communities efforts: Community Action Network has adopted a slightly different nomenclature: social well-being, environmental well-being, and economic well-being.

Table 4.24. Index of Quality of Life

Indices of Quality of life	G_1	G_2	G_3	G_{4*}
Literacy	Illiterate 100.0%	Illiterate 99.0%	Illiterate 80.0% Primary 11.7% Secondary 7.3%	Illiterate 10.0% Primay 46.7% Secondary 23.0% Secondary 10.3%
Health	Epidemics 98.7%	Epidemics 7.7% More deaths 75.0%	Less death 81.7% Less births 13.0%	Less deaths 23.7% Less births 66.03%
Drinking Water	Open well 100.0%	Open well 23.03% Tank 72.07%	Bore well 77.0% Tap 22.0%	Bore well 68.07% Tap 21.0%
Lighting	Oil lamp 100.0%	Oil lamp 61.03% Kerosene 37.07%	Kerosene 36.0% Electricity 62.0%	Kerosene 13.3% Electricity 76.07%
Fuel	Firewood 100.0%	Firewood 99.03%	Firewood 95.07% Gas 03.03%	Firewood 75.7% Gas 13.03%

* 10 per cent are not considered as they are very young

Social well-being is the satisfaction people experience when they see themselves as part of a compassionate community they have helped create—a community in which all have an opportunity to live a satisfying life, and public and private institutions share with the entire citizenry the responsibility to secure for everyone a humanising education, living wages, public safety, equal justice under the law, environmental protection, and unfettered religious and political participation.

The composite index of social well-being comprises four characteristics. These are social access; social distance; age at marriage and food security. *Social Access* refers to access to Basic amenities and public Institutions such as ration shop, drinking water, Hospital, School, Police station. *Social distance* refers to social distance and social interaction with other communities like ST, SC, BC and OC; *Age at marriage* refers to child marriage, early marriage and right age at marriage; and *food security* refers to Government assistance to food security. The Index consists of a maximum score of 41 points and a minimum score of 11 points. The index is graded into three levels of social well-being such as bad, tolerable and acceptable levels. The result of the analysis is presented in Table 4.25.

Assessment of Levels of Living: Inter-generational Trends

The assessment revealed that generation one and two have really led wretched life in terms of their standard of living, quality of life and social well-being. The only solace was that (36.7%) of subjects in G_2 generation have experienced tolerable social well-being. This is because these members have benefited by the social legislations such as repel of Criminal Tribe Act, Universal Adult Franchise etc.

The scenario has definitely changed during the fourth generation *i.e.,* Respondent's son's generation. 50.33 per cent and 35.0 per cent respectively have been experiencing *good enough* and *satisfactory* levels of standard of living in terms of their livelyhood, food security incomes, housing and assets. On the other hand the third generation (respondents) has been experiencing good enough (72.0%) and not so bad (20.33%) levels of standard of living.

The important feature that has improved the levels of standard of living of these two generations is that of *Stable to very Stable Livelihood* and *Food Security;* followed by improved dwelling conditions. It is true that their incomes have not rised spectacularly and most of them continue to

Table 4.25. Index of Social Well-being

Indices of Social Well-being	G_1	G_2	G_3	G_{4*}
Social Access	No Access 100.0%	No Access 96.0%	Access (98.07)	Access 90.0%
Social Distance	Very bad 98.03%	Very bad 71.07% Bad 27.07%	Very bad 5.0% Bad 47.07% Tolerable 46.0 & Acceptable 1.3%	Bad 1.3% Tolerable 44.7% Acceptable 44.0%
Marriage	Child Marriagc 98.3%	Child Marriage 60.4% 60.4% Early Marraige 38.3%	Early Marriage 74.3% Right Age 25.7%	Early Marriage 5.3% Right Age 84.7%
Food Security government Assistances	No Help 66.3% No resonse 33.7%	No Help 45.7% No response 50.3% Yes 4.0%	Yes 95.0% No response 5.0%	Yes 89.3% No response 0.7%

* 10 per cent are not considered as they are very young.

be poor in terms of their earnings. But the point to be noted is that they have a stable livelyhood which provides them some level of income throughout the year and they have been enjoying *maximum food-security. The assured food security was partly because of stable livelyhood and mostly because of through Government welfare measures namely distribution of subsidised public distribution of rations.* The stable livelyhood mostly refers to basket makings with spilt bamboos and pig-rearing; and few of them indulge in white collar and business activities. Agriculture and related manual activities have not helped these sections and on the other hand these sections have shown greater flair for micro entrepreneurial activities.

Our assessment reveals that respondents' quality of life is Not So Bad (66.33%). This is primarily due to improved healthcare facilities and reduction in mortality, availability of safe drinking water. The fourth generation (respondent's adult sons) have been experiencing relatively better quality of life. Our data shows that (66.66%) of them are experiencing Good Enough level of quality of life and (13.0%) of them have been experiencing *Satisfactory* level of quality of life. This generation in addition to better healthcare, reduction in mortality and birthrates have been experiencing better literacy levels and lighting. Only (10.0%) of subjects of forth generation were illiterates 76.7% have electrified lighting in their dwellings.

The *Social Well-being* of respondents see-sawed between *Tolerable* and *Acceptable* levels. 57.7 per cent of the respondents experienced *Tolerance level of social well-beings.* 42.7 per cent of the respondents are experiencing acceptable level of social well-being. A majority has social access to basic amenities and public institutions with out any social exclusion, improved age at marriage and have received Government assistance for food security. *Notwithstanding these well-being factors what made the difference was levels of social distance and acceptability of the Yerukulas to other communities.* Our data shows that practice of social exclusion still affects the Yerukula respondents. Only (1.3%) respondents have revealed that their social distance and social interaction with non-Yerukula communities is at acceptable level.

On the other hand the assessment of social well-being levels with regard to fourth generation (respondent adult sons) reveals acceptable level of social well-being. All of them have access to public institutions and basic amenities enjoy government assistance of food security. Most of them are married at right age (above 18 years). Their interaction with other communities in terms of social distance is at acceptable

(44.0%) and tolerable (44.7%) levels respectively. In addition members of this generation enjoy the support and patronage of their parents and perhaps their parents-in-law too. (Table 4.26)

Table 4.26. Social assessment of standard of living, quality of life and social well-being of Yerukulas

Indices of	G_1	G_2	G_3	G_4*
Standard of living	Very Bad 100.0%	Not so Bad 91.0%	Not So 20.33% Good Enough 72.0%	Good Enough 50.33% Satisactory 35.0%
Quality of life	Very Bad 100.0%	Bad 91.0%	Not So Bad 66.33%	Good Enough 66.66% Satisactory 13.0%
Social well-being	Bad 100.0%	Bad 62.3% Tolerable 36.7%	Tolerable 57.7% Acceptable 42.7%	Acceptable 87.3% 87.3%

* 10% of the total is not considered as they are very young.

The assessment reveals the progressively changing trends in the levels of living of Yerukula tribe in Rayalaseema region. The standard of living of Yerukulas have certainly bettered from the pre-Independence days. The social stigma has greatly declined through not erased completely and there is an increasing trend of social inclusion. (See Table 4.27)

But the sad and trite fact is that they still continue to be poor, less literate of not illiterate, dependent on the mercy of the welfare programmes for food security and are continued to be socially excluded in certain vital arenas like educational attainment and occupation.

It's true that they do not experience agonising lives of their forefathers and fathers. But it is also equally true that they are yet to attain equality of opportunity and the cent per cent Acceptable level of Social Well-being and Social Belonging. Yerukulas and as well as the Nation Builder leaders, therefore have a long march ahead.

The Yerukulas are balancing their lives on such precarious and notionally stable vocation as basket-making with split bamboos and pig-rearing which is like a water bubble. In the context and advent of Globalisation, Yerukulas need to be prepared and be provided with new skills so as to avoid a plunge in to abyss and lose what they have gained. Yerukulas and such other semi-nomadic socially excluded communities (not the ex-untouchables) need to be provided with focussed attention.

Being semi-nomadic and a tribe of plains, the Scheduled Tribe status has not really benefited the Yerukulas of Rayalaseema.

Table 4.27. Yerukulas: Social Stigma
Social Exclusion and Inclusion

Indices	G_1	G_2	G_3	G_4
Lively hood	Very uns-table 59.0% stable 41.0%	stable 100.0%	stable 81.33%	Very stable 18.33% Stable 21.0% Seasonal 41.33%
Found Security	Often starved 100.0%	Often starved 37.0% Food was scarce 53.0%	Not Misseo meals 36.7% Meals twice a day 61.0%	Meals twice/ thrice a day 89.3%
Food Security government Assistances	No Help 66.3% No response 33.7%	No Help 45.7% No response 50.3% Yes 4.0%	Yes 95.0% No response 5.0%	Yes 89.3% No response 0.7%
Assets	Pigs/Fowl 100.0%	Pigs/Fowl 98.3%	Pigs & Movable 32.6%	Movable + Immovable

...(Contd.)

Indices	**G_1**	**G_2**	**G_3**	**G_4**
			Movable + Immovable 34.3% Costly items 13.6% Nil 4.8	20.3% Costly items 34.0% Nil 5.0%
Literacy	Illiterate 100.0%	Illiterate 99.0%	Illiterate (80.0) Primary (11.7) Secondary (7.3)	Illiterate 10.0% Primary 46.7% Secondary 23.0% Above Secondary 10.3%
Health	Epidemics 98.7%	Epidemics 7.7% More deaths 75.0%	Less death (81.7) Less births (13.00)	Less deaths 23.7% Less births 66.03%
Drinking Water	Open well 100.0%	Open well 23.03% Tank 72.07%	Bore-well (77.00) Tap (22.00)	Bore-well 68.07% Tap 21.0%
Social Access to Public Facilities School, Hospital, Ration shop, Police Station Drinking water	No Access 100.0%	No Access 96.00%	Access (98.07)	Access 90.0%
Social Distance	Very bad 98.03%	Very bad 71.07% Bad 27.0%	Very bad 5.0% Bad 47.0% 46.0% Acceptable (1.3%)	Bad (1.3% Tolerable 44.7% Accepable 44.0
Marriage	Child Marriage 98.3%	Child Marriage 60.4% Early Marriage 38.3%	Early Marriage 74.3% Right Age (25.7%)	Early Marriage 5.3% Right Age 84.7%
Social stigma	Strong	Strong	Weak	Declined

REFERENCES

Agarwal, D.K. and K.N. Agarwal, 1987 'Early Childhood Mortality in Bihar and Uttar Pradesh', *Indian Paediatrics* 24, No.8 (August): 627-32.

Aras, R., N. Pai, and A. Purandare, 1990. 'Perinatal mortality—A Retrospective Hospital Study', *Journal of Obstetrics and Gynaecology* 40, No.3 (June), 365-69.

Atkinson, A.B. (1998), "Social Exclusion, Poverty and Unemployment," in: A.B. Atkinson and J. Hills (eds.), *Exclusion, Employment and Opportunity,* CASE/4, Centre for Analysis of Social Exclusion, London School of Economics, 1–20.

Atkinson, A.B., B. Cantillon, E. Marlier and B. Nolan (2002), *Social Indicators: The EU and Social Inclusion,* Oxford University Press, Oxford.

Bhatia, J.C. 1988. 'A Study of Maternal Mortality in Anantapur District, Andhra Pradesh, India' Bangalore: Indian Institute of Management.

Chatterjee, Meera. 1989, 'Socio-economic and Socio-cultural Influences on Women's Nutritional Status Roles' in C. Gopalan and Suminer Kaur (eds), *Women and Nutrition in India,* New Delhi: Nutrition Foundation of India.

Dawn, C.S. and Bani Kumar Mitra. 1990. 'Effect of Food Supplementation on Maternal Weight Gain, Low Birth Weight Incidence, Infant Weight Gain and Breast Feed Performance', *Journal of Obstetrics and Gynaecology* 40, No.3 (June): 313-18.

Department of Education (2006) *Sarva Shiksha Abhiyan: Fourth Joint Review Mission.*Aide Memoire, New Delhi.

Enthoven, R.E., "The Tribes and Castes of Bombay", (Bombay: Government of Central Press 1922), Vol.II, p.267.

Furar, C.V., Haimendorf, *"The Tribes of India, The Struggle of Survival",* Oxford University Press, Delhi, 1982.

Hassan, S.S., *"Castes and Tribes of the H. E. H The Nizams Dominions Hyderabad State* Bombay, (Government Central Press 1920) pp. 185-95.

Jain, M.L. and Dinesh Agarwal. 1986. 'Utilisation of Maternal Services in an ICDS Block', *Journal of Obstetrics and Gynaecology* 36, N.5(October): 842-44.

Jorge Lara-Braud, 1999 Chair COMMUNITY ACTION NETWORK Community Council Josh Wolfe, *International Council on Local Environmental Initiatives* 2000.

K.S. Singh, *"Indian Communities,"* Oxford University press, Delhi 1998.

Kamat, A.R., 1982, Education and Social Change, *Economic and Political Weekly.*

Kanitkar, Tara and R.K. Sinha, 1989. 'Ante-natal Care Services in Five States of India'. In S.N. Singh, M.K. Premi, P.S./ Bhatia and Ashish Bose (eds.), *Population Transition in India,* Vol.2, pp.201-11, Delhi: B.R. Publishing Corporation.

Kapil, U., 1990. "Promotion of Safe Motherhood in India," *Indian Paediatrics,* 27: No.3 (March), pp. 232-238.

Khan, M.E. and C.V.S. Prasad, 1983. *Under-utilisation of Health Services in Rural India: A Comparative Study of Bihar, Gujarat and Kerala,* Baroda: Operations Research Group.

Khan, M.E., Richard Anker, S.K. Ghosh Dastidar and Sashi Airathi. 1988. 'Inequalities Between Men and Women in Nutrition and Family Welfare Services: An In-depth Equiry in an Indian Village', *Social Action* 38 (OctoberDecember).

Kumar, Harsh, S. Aneja, V.K. Prasad, S.K. Arora and D.N. Mulick. 1988. 'Tetanus Neonatorum: Clinico-epidemiological Profile', *Indian Paediatrics* 25 No.11 (November), 1054-1057.

Lalitha, V., *"The making of Criminal Tribes,"* Pattern and Transition, New Era Publication Madras, 1995.

Mathai, Sharmma, T. 1989, 'Women and the Health System' in C. Gopalan and Suminder Kaur(Eds.), *Women and Nutrition in India*, New Delhi, Nutrition Foundation of India.

Meena Radha Krsihna, "The Criminal Tribe Act in Madras Presidency," Implication for Itinerant Trading Communities, *The Indian Economic and Social History Review*, 26, 3, Sage, New Delhi 1989.

Mehta, A. and K. Jayant. 1981. 'Parinatal Mortality Survey in India (1977-79) Part I, Identification of Health Intervention Needs', *Journal of Obstetric Gynaecology* 32, No.2(April), 183-215.

Mehta, A. M.E. Khan, R.B. Gupta, M.M. Gandotra and O.S. Ojha. 1983. *'Role of Health Services Delivery on Acceptance of Family Planning,* New Delhi: ICMR, Mimeo.

Mohan Rao, K., *"Tribes of Andhra Pradesh,"* 1998, TCR, and TI, Hyderabad

Mr. Michael Jacobs Fabian Society, 11 Dartmouth Street, London, SW1H 9BN October 1994 - September 1996.

Murthy, G.V., Anil Goswami and Saroja Narayanan. 1990. 'Utilisation Patterns of Ante-natal Services in an Urban Slum', *Journal of Obestetrics and Gynaecology* 40, No.1 (February), 42-46.

Nagaraju, K. 2007. 'Dalits and Adolescent Sexual Health: Issues and Practices: A Study of De-notified Tribes, Scheduled Castes and Backward Caste Communities in Andhra Pradesh', *Paper Presented to the Workshop for Young Social Scientists,* Jammu.

Nana Bapat, 1961, Tribal Education—A Problem, *Vanyajati.*

Narendra Kumar Das Gupta, 1963, *Problems of Tribal Education* and the Santhals, New Delhi.

Papa Rao Naidu M, 1905, *History of Railway Thieves,* Madras.

Ramachandran, Prema., 1989. 'Lactation-nutrition-fertility Interaction', in C. Gopalan and Sluminder Kaur (Eds.), *Women and Nutrition in India,* New Delhi, Nutrition Foundation of India.

Ramalinga Swami, V. 1985. 'The State of Life' *Report of the National Seminar on Reducing Incidence of Low Birth Weight Babies in India,* New Delhi: National Institute of Public Cooperation and Child development.

Royston, Eric and Sue Armstrong. 1989. *'Preventing Maternal Deaths',* Geneva: World Health Organisation.

Sadik, Jafis, 1980. *'Family Planning: Improving the Health of Women',* Draper Fund Report, 9 (October).

Sharma, N. and P. Bali. 1989. 'A Comparative Study of Maternal Mortality and Morbidity in a Teaching Hospital of Northern India', *Journal of Obstetric and Gynecology*, 38, No. 2, p. 177-181.

Shashi.S.S. 1995, *Tribes of Andhra Pradesh.* Anmol Publications Pvt Ltd New Delhi.

Simhadir, Y.S., 1976, Changing Criminal behaviour of an ex-Criminal Tribe in an Indian Village, *Indian Journal of Criminology.*

Singh Meharban. And V.K. Paul. 1988. 'Strategies to Reduce Perinatal and Neonatal Mortality', *Indian Paediatrics* 23, No.6 (June): 499-509.

Singh, Meharban. 1986. 'Hospital-based Data on Perinatal and Neonatal Mortality in India,' Indian Paediatrics 23, No.8 (August) 579-584.

Singh, Surinder, Jagieet Singh, Sushila Mittal, R.K.D. Goel, Tejbir Singh and S.K. Oberoi. 1988. 'A Study of Ante-natal Services in Rural Areas of District of Bathinda of Punjab', *Journal of Obstetrics and Gynaecology* 38, No.1 (February); 2-26.

Sokhy, J. 1988. 'Magnitude of problems in India', in Ministry of Health and Family Welfare, *The Control of Neonatal Tetanus in India,* pp. 16-23, New Delhi, Government of India, quoted in Singh and Paul.

Srikantia, S.G. 1989a. 'Nutritional Deficiency Diseases', in C. Gopalan and Suminder Kaur (eds), *Women and Nutrition in India,* New Delhi: Nutrition Foundation of India.

Starrs, Ann and Diane Measham. 1990, *'Challenge for the Nineties: Safe Motherhood in South Asia',* New York and Washington: The World Bank and Family Care International.

Thurston, E., *"Castes and Tribes of Southern India,"* Madras Government Press. 1909 rpt. 1975, Delhi Cosmo Publication Vol. 111, pp. 442-3.

Tripathi, A.M. D.K. Agarwarl, K.N. Agarwal, R.R. Devi and S. Cherian. 1987. 'Nutritional Status of Rural Pregnant Women and Foetal Outcome', *Indian Paediatrics 24,* No.9 (September): 703-712.

Umamohan, C. A. Naganna, Educational Attainments and Empowerment of a Stigmatised Scheduled Tribe: An Inter-generational Study of Yerukula Tribe in Rayalaseema. *Paper Presented to the National Seminar, Education and Social Empowerment,* 5th & 6th July 2007, Dr. B. R. A. Open University, Hyderabad.

Umamohan, C. A. Naganna, Nagaraju,K. Perception and Assessment on Standard of Living, Quality of Life and Social Well-being: An Inter-generational Study of a Stigmatised Scheduled Tribe, the Yerukulas in Rayalaseema Region of Andhra Pradesh, *National Seminar on Tribal Development: A Myth or Pragmatic Reality?* 26th and 27th February, 2007. Organised by Department of Anthropology, Sri Venkateswara University, Tirupati

Umamohan, C.1983 "Occupational Change and Mobility Trends: A Study of Two Villages in Andhra Pradesh, *Unpublished Ph.D Thesis Submitted to Osmania University,* Hyderabad.

Umamohan, Ch., A. Naganna, K. Nagaraju, 2007. *Reproductive Health Care: Intergenerational Study of Yerukala Tribe in Rayalaseema Region,* in NOMADS, Prof. B.S. Vasudeva Rao (ed), Andhra University Press, Visakhapatnam, Andhra Pradesh, pp.130-137.

Umamohan,C; Venkataramana,G; Naganna, A., "Yerukula Tribes and Social Transformation," Bharatiya Adimajathi Sevak Sangh (*Vanyagati*), New Delhi 2006.

UNICEF, India. 1991, *'Children and Women in India: A Situation Analysis,'* New Delhi, UNICEF.

Summary and Conclusion

The present study is an attempt to study the social transformation of Yerukula community. Yerukula is a primitive tribal community. It carries a social stigma as a criminal tribe. The social transformation of this community is examined in the *conceptual framework of social exclusion and inclusion* with reference to change and continuity in the areas of livelihood opportunities (occupational changes); educational levels; healthcare access; social stigma—social exclusion and inclusion.

The study is carried out in the context Rayalaseema region of Andhra Pradesh.

OBJECTIVES

1. To review the Tribal Development Programmes in India;
2. To portray the socio-economic status of the Yerukula community;
3. To examine the change and continuity in livelihood opportunities; levels of education; and access to health care; and
4. To analyse the process of social exclusion and social inclusion resulting in social transformation.

METHOD OF STUDY

The universe of the study is Rayalaseema region of Andhra Pradesh. Rayalaseema region comprises four districts *viz.*: Anantapur, Chittor, Kadapa and Kurnool districts. Two districts Anantapur and Kurnool districts were chosen for present study.

A multistage random sampling technique was adopted to draw a representative study sample. Thus, from Anantapur eight habitations of which two urban centers, three semi-urban centers three rural habitations were selected. Similarly one urban center, four semi-urban centers four rural centers from Kurnool district was selected. Our study sample constitutes 300 Yerukula households. The sample comprises 85 urban Households, 135 semi-urban households and 80 rural households spread in Kurnool and Anantapur districts of Rayalaseema Region of Andhra Pradesh.

The data was collected from both primary and secondary sources. The primary data was collected by administering structured interview schedule.

The analysis is made with reference to four generations *viz*: Grandfather (G_1), Father (G_2), Respondent (G_3) and Respondent son (G_4) period. The approximate time period of the four generations refer to 1930 for G_1; 1950 for G_2; 1970 for $G_{3;}$ and 1990 for G_4 generations.

MAJOR FINDINGS

Socio-economic Characteristics

- The Yerukulas under study represent four endogamous groups. These are Dabba Yerukulas (48.7%) Kunchapu Yerukulas (27.3%) Eeta Yerukula (19%) and Nulaka Yerukula (5%).
- Majority earn an annual income of Rs. 6000 to 12000 thousands. The average income per annum was found to be Rs.7430 with a standard deviation of Rs. 5206. The maximum income earned was Rs. 60,000 per annum.
- Majority of the (97.7%) have nuclear families. And the size of families is 4 to 6 members (64.7%).
- Majority of the (80.3%) were landless and only (19.7%) own marginal and small holdings.

- The average age of the respondents is 45.16 years with a standard deviation of 8.9 years. The youngest respondents was 25 years old and the oldest was 68 years.
- All the Yerukula families under the reference are observed to practice Hindu religion practices. None of the Yerukula families under reference were confined in the rehabitation settlements sponsored by the British Government and the Christian Missionaries during pre-Independence period.
- Our data reveals that (20%) of Yerukula respondent did not vote as they did not have proper identification.
- Our study shows that only 4.7 per cent of the respondents have held any position as office bearers. Only 23.7 per cent have political party affiliations.
- Majority of the respondents (62.7%) reported that they freely participate in social functions. 37.3 per cent reported that they do not participate in social functions. Only 3 per cent reported that they experience social restrictions.

Livelihood Practices

- Our data shows that only 58 per cent of Yerukulas have adhered to traditional callings.
- None of the respondents are representing such traditional occupations like making weavers comb (Kunchepu Yerukula).
- Very small percentage are a involved in fiber rope-making (nulaka) (3.67%).
- Small percentage were found to be involved in mat weaving (mats made of date palm leaves) Etta pulla (16.67)
- A large percentage however, are involved in spilt bamboo weaving (27.67) which is considered to be the vocation of dabba Yerukula; and not all these members belong to dabba Yerukula group.
- 7.6 per cent are involved in pig-rearing.
- 2.3 per cent are involved in dry milch cattle rearing.

- A good percentage (42.00) are found to be involved in other occupations like cultivation, agriculture labour, Business, Auto driving, Moneylending, Bus driver, conductor.

Livelihood Practices: Continuity and Change

- Yerukula do not strictly adhere to their traditionally endogamous occupational callings.
- Further our data also shows that the Yerukula are keen to adopt *and welcome changes in their occupational* callings that would improve their levels of living.
- The percentage of occupation deviation irrespective of sub-group affiliation is found to be 52.00 per cent.
- It is observed that at present the Yerukulas of Rayalaseema are not involved in vending, trading curry leaves, rock salt; transport services; performing Modi; acrobats, or Kunchelu to which they were traditionally associated and are known.

Livelihood Practices: Inter-generational Trends

- Our analysis reveals that during the G_1 and G_2 generations no occupational shifts took place due to structural changes and as such there was no mobility. This period refers to British India and very early decades of Independence.
- The Inter-generational trend shows that the period between G_2 and G_3 the structural mobility occurred was 41.9 per cent took place. 42 per cent of G_3 members were mobile. The exchange mobility was only 0.1 per cent.
- The Intra-generational occupation mobility of G_3 members revealed that 51 per cent were mobile. The minimum structural mobility was 29.35 per cent. But the exchange mobility was 21.65 per cent.
- The inter-generational mobility between G_3 and G_4 reveals that 81.3 per cent of G_4 members were mobile. The minimum structural mobility occurred was 53.96 per cent and the exchange mobility was only 27.34 per cent.

- The intra and inter-generational trends of livelihood practices revealed progressive increase in mobility trends;
- Increasing trends of deviation from parent conferred occupations and traditional occupations.; and
- Progressive inclusive trends into modern occupations;
- The study further reveals that social exclusion persists in equality of opportunities with references to occupational mobility from tradition to modern occupations of higher rank. The lack of educational attainments and requisite modern skills were found to be reason for such an exclusion.

Access to Education

- During the pre-Independence and the early decades of Independence period the Yerukulas experienced total social exclusion with reference to educational opportunities.
- In terms of levels of educational attainments the Yerukulas still experience social exclusion as less than one per cent of Yerukulas under reference have received collegiate level of education.
- As far as access to literacy, the stigmatised tribe of Yerukula is experiencing slow social inclusiveness. But to attain even this, they took five generations of time.
- Yerukulas experience and there still persists social exclusions in terms of gender discrimination, as the female literacy levels are very poor among the Yerukula.
- The levels of educational attainments is very low, it is only up to primary or upper primary level, and less than one per cent of the Yerukulas under reference have received collegiate level of education.
- Child labour persists among Yerukulas; 30 per cent of Yerukula children were involved as child workers and thus they are deprived, denied schooling opportunities and experience social exclusion.

Access to Healthcare

- Birth deliveries during the Grandfather (G_1) and Father (G_2) periods were home deliveries only. Son's generation (G_4) this practice has shifted to institutional deliveries. All the birth deliveries were institutional deliveries. In other words the young Yerukula women have access to institutional services.
- During the G_1 period all the birth deliveries were attended by the untrained elderly women of the community. Yerukulas were deprived of even traditional and semi-professional medical care. But in the case of son's generation (G_4) they were attended by trained nurse (56.8 per cent) and by doctors 43.12 per cent irrespective of rural and urban divide. This indicates access and reach to professional and modern healthcare.
- Only 44.33 per cent of mothers during respondents (G_3) period were immunised whereas 85.87 per cent of Yerukulas young women (G_4) received Tetanus Toxoid injection during the pregnancy 55.66 per cent of women during G_3 period received IFA supplements. Curiously the young Yerukula women (G_4) have shown scant interest in receiving IFA supplements. Only 13.38 per cent of them received Iron Folic Acid tablets.
- During the G_3 generation ante-natal advice was provided by such service providers as Mother 4.7 per cent; untrained elderly woman 1.73 per cent; traditional mid-wife (manthrasani) 1.3 per cent; trained health worker1.3 per cent; ANM/Nurse 83.7 per cent; and doctor 7.3 per cent. During G_4 generation the younger Yerukula women have received this service from only the skilled health professionals such as ANM/Nurse 43.7 per cent; trained health worker 28.0 per cent; and doctor17.7 per cent.
- Post-natal care and services in the case of respondent wives was by mid-wife (0.3 per cent); followed by mothers (26.3 per cent). The remaining majority were attended by the skilled professional health workers like trained health worker((1.0 per cent); ANM/Nurse (54.7 per cent) and doctor (17.7 per cent).Only in the case of 17.66 per

cent doctors services were sought that too in urban and semi-urban areas. Against this scenario in the case of younger Yerukulas women (G_4), the post-natal care and services were offered by doctor (51.7 per cent) followed by ANM/Nurse (32.3 per cent) 0.4 per cent by trained health worker.

- Our data reveals that still births were as high as 31.7 per cent during respondent's (G_3) period. This was reduced to only 4.6 per cent during son's generation (G_4) period. Obviously this is due to better ante and post-natal care and services as well as immunisation of expectant mothers and due to institutional deliveries. However, abortions reported were fewer (5.3 per cent) during respondent's period as against 24.7 per cent during son's generation. The other delivery problems too were less during respondent generation (8.7 per cent) as against 12.00 per cent during son's period. These low figures of the respondent period presumably due to under reporting.
- There is appreciable reduction in neo-natal infant and maternal mortality incidents from G_1 generation to G_4 generation.
- The neo-natal mortality incidents were fewer in G_1 and G_2 generations (13.7 and 25.7 per cent respectively). It was highest in G_3 generation (46.3 per cent) which was brought down to 36.01 per cent in G_4 generation.
- Similarly infant mortality incidents were reduced from 61 per cent to 31.3 per cent.
- However, the incidence of maternal mortality was high during G_1 and G_2 generations (55.3 and 29.7 per cent) and this was brought down to 11.3 per cent during G4 generation.
- Majority of the respondents (82.7 per cent) have acknowledged that neo-natal and infant mortality and maternal mortality incidents among them were reduced in the last five years irrespective of rural urban divide.
- The following reasons were attributed for this reduction. Better child healthcare (17.3 per cent); good environment (5.6 per cent); better medical facilities (11.3 per cent);

Provision of medical care (18.3 per cent); and timely vaccines (10.3).

- The practice of breast feeding the infant is rather declining in the case of younger Yerukula women. 47 per cent of young women depend upon other sources such as cow/buffalo milk; milk-powder.

Stigma—Social Exclusion and Social Inclusion

- Assessment of levels of living revealed that generation one and two have really led wretched life in terms of their standard of living, quality of life and social well-being.
- The only solace was that (36.7%) of subjects in G_2 generation have experienced *Tolerable* Social well-being.
- The scenario has definitely changed during the fourth generation *i.e.,* Respondent's son's generation. 50.33 per cent and 35.0 per cent respectively have been experiencing *good enough* and *satisfactory* levels of standard of living in terms of their livelyhood, food security incomes, housing and assets.
- On the other hand the third generation (respondents) has been experiencing good enough (72.0%) and not so bad (20.33%) levels of standard of living.
- The assured food security was partly because of stable livelyhood and mostly because of through Government welfare measure namely distribution of subsidised public distribution of rations.
- The stable livelyhood mostly refers to basket makings with spilt bamboos and pig-rearing; and few of them indulge in white collar and business activities.
- Agriculture and related manual activities have not helped these sections and on the other hand these sections have shown greater flair for micro entrepreneurial activities.
- Our assessment reveals that respondent's quality of life is Not So Bad (66.33%).

- The fourth generation (respondent's adult sons) have been experiencing relatively better quality of life. Our data shows that (66.66%) of them are experiencing *Good Enough* level of quality of life and (13.0%) of them have been experiencing *Satisfactory* level of quality of life.
- The 4th generations in addition to better healthcare, reduction in mortality and birthrates have been experiencing better literacy levels and lighting. Only (10.0%) of subjects of fourth generation were illiterates 76.7 per cent having electrified lighting in their dwellings.
- The *Social Well-being* of respondents see-sawed between *Tolerable* and *Acceptable* levels. 57.7 per cent of the respondents experienced *Tolerable level of social well-beings.*
- 42.7 per cent of the respondents are experiencing *Acceptable* level of social well-being.
- A majority have social access to basic amenities and public institutions with out any social exclusion, improved age at marriage and have received Government assistance for food security.
- Notwithstanding these well-being factors what made the difference was low levels of social distance and acceptability of the Yerukulas to other communities.
- Our data shows that practice of social exclusion still affects the Yerukula respondents. Only (1.3%) respondents have revealed that their social distance and social interaction with non-Yerukula communities is at acceptable level.
- On the other hand the assessment of social well-being levels with regard to fourth generation (respondent adult sons) reveals acceptable level of social well-being. All of them have access to public institutions and basic amenities enjoy government assistance of food security.
- Most of them (G_4) were married at right age (above 18 years). Their interaction with other communities in terms of social distance is at acceptable (44.0%) and tolerable (44.7%) levels respectively. In addition members of this

generation enjoy the support and patronage of their parents and perhaps their parents-in-laws too.

- The assessment reveals the progressively changing trends in the levels of living of Yerukula tribe in Rayalaseema region.
- The levels of living of Yerukulas have certainly bettered from the pre-Independence days. The social stigma has greatly declined though not erased completely and there is an increasing trends of social inclusion.
- But the sad and trite fact is that they still continue to be poor, less literate if not illiterate, dependent on the mercy of the welfare programmes for food security and are continued to be socially excluded in certain vital areas like educational attainment and occupation.
- It is observed that they do not experience agonising lives of their fore fathers and fathers. But the study also reveals that they are yet to attain equality of opportunity and higher levels of social inclusion. Acceptable level of social well being and social belonging. Yerukulas and as well as the nation builder leaders, therefore have a long march ahead.

CONCLUSION

Based on the analysis discussion and findings of the study made to draw the following broad conclusions with regard to social transformation of Yerukulas with reference to change and continuity in the above of livelihood and access to education and healthcare.

Our first conclusion is that the Yerukulas over a period of four generation have undergone transformation in the pursuits of livelihoods. They have abandoned their criminal activities as a change source of livelihood. They are now more or less leading sedentary settled life. Most of them do not adhere to parent/tradition conferred occupations and are steadily, slowly making are entry into modern occupations. They now exhibit flair for entrepreneurial activities. The lack of better levels of educational attainments and requisites modern skills is are inhibiting factor for their further social transformation and entry into modern occupational structure. The increasing trends of occupational deviations from traditional/parent conferred occupations, inter and intra generational occupational mobility trends, the minimum structural (occupational) mobility and the exchange mobility occurred over the four generations support this conclusion.

Our second conclusion is that the Yerukula are not for literacy promotions. The increasing levels of literacy over the four generations is a testimony this. But poverty, poor incomes and certain occupational persists the basket weaving, pig-rearing have stinted female literacy and encouraged child labour, and low levels of educational attainments.

Our third conclusion is that the Yerukulas are not overse to modern healthcare and services. In feel they have not access to modern healthcare and services but most of them are availing these services. The high levels of institutional birth deliveries and professional attendance at the time of birth delivery, decreasing trends of mortality, neo-natal, infant and maternity is a poor for these.

Our fourth and fifth conclusion is that the Yerukulas, the members of ex-criminal tribe, are now no longer shunned and socially excluded.

Unlike in the previous generations, the present day Yerukulas have been benefited by social inclusion. The social stigma of criminal tribe though not erased completely, they now have better social interaction, greater social participation, better standard of living, quality of life and social well-being, relative to their previous generations. However, social exclusion persists in the areas of better levels of educational attainments, modern occupational skills for want of focussed attention. The tribal development programmes have not benefited Yerukulas, a tribe settled in plain areas.

SELECT BIBLIOGRAPHY

Agrawal, Grisrish and Colin Gonsalves (2005), *Dalit and the Law,* Human Right Law Netwok, Delhi.

Alam, J.1989: *'Tribal Identity in Jharkhand'*, in P.C.Chatterji(ed): *Self Image Identity and Nationality* (42-56). Shimla: Indian Institute of Advanced Study.

Alam, J.1989: *'Tribal Identity in Jharkhand',* in P.C.Chatterji(ed): *Self Image Identity and Nationality* (42-56). Shimla: Indian Institute of Advanced Study.

Albrow, Martin. 1996. The *Global Age*. Cambridge: Polity.

Ali Raza Mossvi (2001), Rural Development Through JFM: A Case Study, in G.P. Misra and B.K. Bajpai (Ed.), *Community Participation in Natural Resource Management,* Rawat Publications, Jaipur, p. 293.

Ambedkar B.R. (first Published 1987), "Philosophy of Hindism" Vasant Moon (Edit) *"Dr. Babasaheb Ambedkar Writings and Speeches"* Vol.3 Page 1-94.

Ambedkar B.R. (first published 1987), "The Hindu Social Order - Its Essential Features" in Vasant Moon (Edit), *"Dr. Babasaheb Ambedkar Writing and Speeches",* Vol. 3, pp. 95-115, Deptt. of Education, Govt. of Maharashtra, Bombay.

Ambedkar, B.R. (first published 1987) "The Hindu Social Orde—Its Unique Features" in Vasant Moon (Edit) *"Dr. Babasaheb Ambedkar Writings and Speeches"* Vol. 3, pp. 116-129, Deptt. of Education, Govt. of Maharashtra, Bombay.

Aparna Mahanta 1994. Article *The Indian State and Patriarchy,* p. 88.

Arnold, D.1982. : *'Rebellious Hillman: Gudem – Rampa prising 1839-1924',* In Ranjit Guha (ed): Subaltern Studies I. Delhi: Oxford University Press.

Ashish Kothari (2001), Towards Participatory, Conservation in India: National Scenario and Lessons from Field, in G.P. Misra and B.K. Bajpai (Ed.), *Community Participation in Natural Resource Management,* Rawat Publication, Jaipur, p. 172.

Behure, N.K., 1995, "Tribes in India: Planned Development" in Amar Kumar Singh and M.K. Jabbi (ed), *Tribals in India: Development Deprivation and Discontent,* Council for Social Development, New Delhi.

Belshaw, Cyrill S. 1972. 'Development: The Contribution of Anthropology', *International Social Science Journal,* 24(6): 41-65. 1977. 'The Contribution of Anthropologist to development'.

Bhattacharjee, S.R.1989. *Tribal Insurgency in Tripura: A Study in the Exploration of Causes.* New Delhi: Inter-India Publications.

Bose, A. 1990. *Tribal Demography and Development in North-Eastern India.* Tiplut Nongbri and Delhi: B.R.Publishing Corporation.

Bose, N.K.1941. 'The Hindu Method of Tribal Absorption', *Science and Culture,* (7): 188-94.

Brass, P. 1991. Ethnicity and Nationalism: Theory and Comparison. New Delhi: Sage Publications.

Burman, Roy. B.K. 1972. 'Integrated Area Approach to the Problems of the hill Tribes of North-East India ', in K.S.Singh (ed): *The Tribal Situation in India* (67-102). Shimla: Indian Institute of Advanced Study.

Burman, Roy.B.K.1986. *Challenges of Development and Tribal Women in India.* Udaipur: M.L.V.Tribal Research and Training Institute.

Chaube, S.C.1973. *Hill Politics in North-East India*. New Delhi: Orient Longman.

Chaudhuri, B. (ed).1982 'Introduction', in Buddhadeb Chaudhuri (ed): *Tribal Development in India* (XVII-XXXVI). New Delhi: Inter-India Publications.

Chaudhuri, B. 1992. *Ethnopoitics and Identity Crisis*. Delhi: Inter India Publications.

Danda, A.K.1973. *Tribal Economy and Their Transformation*. New Delhi: I.C.S.S.R.

Das Gupta, L.R., 1998, "Health Care", Vol. 42, No. 4, *Yojana*. Encyclopaedia of Indian Tribes.

Data, P.S.1993. *Autonomy Movements in Assam*. Delhi: Omsons Publishers.

Deller, Steven C. and Nelson, Carl H; Measuring the Economic Efficiency of Producing Rural Road Services, American Journal of Agricultural Economics 73 (1), 1991 (February: 1994-2002).

Deniroff, R. 1974. *The Sociology of Dissent*. New York: Hardcourth Bruce Serge Ja Vanovich.

Deshpande, Sukhadeo Thorat, Harsh Mander and Amita Baviskar and Research and other Regional Staff, Delhi (ongoing study).

Dhar, T.N., 2001, "Land and Water Resources in Indian Himalayas: Issues of Development, Uses, Sustainability and People's Dimension", in G.P.Mishra, et.al., (ed) *'Community Participation in Natural Resource Management'*, Rawath publications, Jaipur.

Dommen, A.G.1967. 'Separatist Tendencies in Eastern India ', *Asian Survey*, 7 (10): 726-39.

Dubey, S.M.1982. 'Inter-ethnic Alliance, Tribal Movements and Integration in North-east India', in K.S.Singh (ed): *Tribal Movements in India*, Vol.I (8-19). New Delhi: Manohar.

Dutta, L. 1985. 'Violence in India: The Case of Naga National Movement', *Economic and Political Weekly*, 16(24): 1053-55.

Duyker, E. 1987. *Tribal Guerillas: The Santhals of West Bengal and the Naxalite Movement*. Delhi: Oxford University Press.

Enthoven, R.E., *"The Tribes and Castes of Bombay"*, (Bombay: Government of Central Press 1922), Vol. II, p. 267.

Evaluation of Akshara Sankranthi Programme, Khammam District, (2001).Institute of Development Research and Alternatives, 518, Balaji Colony, Tirupati – 517 502.

Fuchs, S. 1965. *Rebellions Prophet: A Study of Messianic Movements in India*, Bombay.

Furar, C.V., Haimendorf, *"The Tribes of India, The Struggle of Survival"*, Oxford University press, Delhi, 1982.

Gough, K. 1979. 'Indian Peasant Uprisings', in A.R.Desai (ed): *Peasant Struggles in India* (85-126). Bombay: Oxford University Press.

Government of India, 1986, National Policy on Education, New Delhi.

Government of India, 2003, *Tenth Five Year Plan 2003-07*, New Delhi.

Govinda, R. (Ed) 2002, *Indian Education Report,* New Delhi. Oxford University Press.

Guha, A.1979. 'Great Nationalism, Little Nationalism and Problem of Integration: A Tentative View', *Economic and Political Weekly,* 14(7-8):455-78.

Guha, R. 1989b. 'Saboteurs in The Forest: Colonialism and Peasant Resistance in the Indian Himalaya', in Forrest D.Colburn (ed): *Everyday Forms of Peasant Resistance.* New Delhi: M.E. Sharpe.

Guha, R.1989a. *The Unquiet Wood: Ecological Change and Peasant Resistance in Himalaya.* Delhi: Oxford University Press.

Guha, Ranajit. 1983c. *Elementary Aspects of Peasant Insurgency in Colonial India.* Delhi: Oxford University Press.

H.M.Mathur (ed): *Anthropology in Development Process* (45-62). New Delhi: Vikas Publishing House.

Hassan, S.S., *"Castes and Tribes of the H. E. H The Nizams Dominions Hyderabd State Bombay,* (Government Central Press 1920), pp. 185-95.

Hiramani, A.B., *"Health Educattion in Primary Healthcare",* B.R. Publishing Corporation, New Delhi.

Hussain, M. 1987. 'Tribal Movements for an Autonomous State in Assam', *Economic and Political Weekly*, 32(3):1329-32.

Imchen, C.L. (1990). 'Issues in Tribal Development', in Ashis Bose, Tiplut Nongbri and Niklesh Kumar (ed): *Tribal Demography and Development in North-Eastern India* (40-46). Delhi: B.R. Publishing Corporation.Karma, M.N. 1998. *Social Movements in North-East India*. New Delhi: Indus Publishing Company.

K.S. Singh, *"Indian Communities,"* Oxford University Press, Delhi 1998.

Kabeer, Naila, 2006, Social Exclusion and the MDGs: The Challeange of Durable Inequalities in the Asian Context, Institute of Development Studies *Paper Presented at the 2015 Conference.*

Lakshmaiah, T., "Tribal Development: Need to Evolve People Oriented Approach", *Kurukshetra*, Vol. 50, No. 2, December 2001.

Lal Deepak (1984) "Hindu Equalibrium", *Cultural Stability and Economic Stagnation,* Vol. I Carendor, 1988 Oxford

Link, B. G., and J. C. Phelan (2001): "Conceptualising Stigma," *Annual Review of Sociology,* 27, 363–85.

Mahendra Dev. S. (2001), Village Institutions and Common Property Resources: Social Economic Impact and Lessons for Tree Growers Cooperatives, in G.P. Misra and B.K. Bajpal (ed.), *Community Participation in Natural Resource Management,* Rawat Publications, Jaipur, p. 225.

Mahipal 1998. Women in Panchayat Experienced of a Training Camp, *Economic and Political Weekly,* January 24-1998.

Mahpatra, L.K. 1972. 'Social Movements Among Tribes of India ', in K.S.Singh (ed): *The Tribal Situation in India* (371-81). Shimla: Indian Institute of Advanced Study.

Mayra Buvnic (2005) *Social Exclusion in Latin Aamerica*, in Mayara Buvinic and Jacqueline.

Mazza and Ruthanne Deutsch (2005) *"Social Inclusion and Economic Development in Latin Aamerica,* Inter-Aamerican Development Bank, Newyork.

Meena Radha Krsihna, "The Criminal Tribe Act in Madras Presidency," Implication for Itinerant Trading Communities, *The Indian Economic and Social History Review,* 26, 3, Sage, New Delhi 1989.

Mohan Rao, K., *"Tribes of Andhra Pradesh,"* 1998, TCR, and TI, Hyderabad.

Mohanti, Neeti, 1997, *"Tribal Policy in India"* in Bupendra Singh and Neeli Mohanti ed.), New Delhi, Inter-India Publications.

Mukherjee R.K., "Self-help Groups and Bank Linkages", *The Economic Times,* 26 May 1999.

Nag, C.R. 1993. *Mizo Society in Transition.* New Delhi: Vikas Publishing House.

Naganna, A. Globalisation, Education and Occupational Changes: A Study of Stigmatised Scheduled Tribe – The Yerukulas. *Paper Presented Workshop for Young Social Scientists,* 5 & 6 October. Jammu University.

Nancaraiah.G.2000, "Economic Development of Scheduled Castes", in Chandu Subbarao *et.al., 'Development of Weaker Sections',* Rawath Publications, Jaipur.

Navalalkha, S. (1959). 'The Authority Structure Among the Bhumji and the Bhils: A Study of Historic Causations', *The Eastern Anthropologist,* 13(1): 27-40.

Nuthara, C. 1996. *Mizoram: Society and Polity.* New Delhi: Indus Publishing Company.

Office of the Registrar General, India, 2005.

Oommen, T.K. 1981. 'Social Movements, National Crisis and Social Change—The Indian Situation', *NERC Bi-Annual Journal of Social Sciences,* 1:1-17.

Oommen, T.K. 1990. *Protest and Change: Studies in Social Movements.* New Delhi: Sage Publications.

Padmanabham, B.S., 2000, "Health Care: Challenges", Vol.44, No.2, Yojan.

Panda Saumay, 2001, "Appropriate Technology in Health" *Bharatiya Samajik Chintan*, A Quarterly Journal of Social Sciences, Nos.1-4, Vol.XXIV.

Parthsarathy G, *Economic Impact of Women's Thrift and Credit Societies,* Institute; of Development Planning Studies, Visakhapatnam, 1995.

Pathy, J. 1998. 'Impact of Development Projects on Yribals', in Vidut Joshi (ed): *Tribal Situation in India: Issues in Development* (275-86). New Delhi: Rawat Publications.

Paul, M.C. 1989. *Dimensions of Tribal Movements in India: A Study of Udayachal in Assam Valley.* New Delhi: Inter-India Publications.

Planning Commission, 2006. *Towards Faster and More Inclusive Growth: An Approach to the 11th Five Year Plan,* Government of India, New Delhi.

Pradip K.Bhowmick, 1995, "Tribal Development under Similar Ecology", in Amar Kumar Singh and M.K.Jabbi, (Ed), *Tribals in India: Development, Deprivation and Discontent,* Council for Social Development, New Delhi.

Prasada Rao M, (2004) *'Information About the Lives and Living Conditions of Savara and Jathapu Tribes' in 'Information, Communication, Library and Community Development'* Vol. I Ed. Ramesh Babu B. and Gopalakrishna, S,B R. Publishing Corporation, Delhi.

Pratap, D.R. 1982. 'Approach to Tribal Development', in Buddadeb Chaudhury (ed): *Tribal Development in India.* New Delhi: Inter India Publication.

Raghaviah, V. 1979. 'Tribal Revolts in Chronological Order: 1778 to 1971', in A.R. Desai (ed): *Peasant Struggles in India* (23-27). Bombay: Oxford University Press.

Raj, D.Sunder, 2000, "People's Participation and Rural Development", *Kurukshetra*, Vol. 48, No. 5, February.

Raj, D.Sunder, 2003, "Tribal Community Development: A Participatory Approach", *Third Concept,* Vol.17, No.195, May.

Ramachandren, Vimala (ed) 2004, *Gender and Social Equity in Primary Education Hierarchies of Access*, Sage Publications, India Private Limited. New Delhi.

Ramana Rao, D.V.V.,: Self-help Groups: A Course Study of Voluntary Organisations, *Research Highlights* 1997-98, NIRD, Hyderabad

Rao, K.Mohan, 1998, "Towards Understanding Culture of Tribal Communities in India". *Man in India*, Vol.78 (1&2), March-June.

Rao, M.S.A. (ed). 1979. *Social Movements in India*, Vol. 1, New Delhi: Manohar Publications.

Ray, A. 1982. *Mizoram: Dynamics of Change*. Calcutta: Pearl Publishers.

Reddy, K.N., and Tripathy, K.K., 1991, "Priorities in Resources Allocation for Healthcare in India: A Basic Needs Approach", *Asian Economic Review* 33 (2), 177-204.

Rotter-Hogan, e. 1982. 'Insurrection or Ostracism: A Study of Santhal Rebellion of 1855', Contributions to Indian Sociology, 16(1): 79-96.

Roy Burman *et.al.,* (2002): A Glimpse into Self-help in Tribal Areas, *Journal of the Indian Anthropological Society* 37 (2), 113-121 July.

Sareen, H.K. 1980. *Insurgency in North-East: A Study of Sino-American Role.* New Delhi; Sterling Publishers.

Sen Amrty, 2000. *Social Exclusion: Concept Application and Scrutiny.* Office of Environment and Social Development, Asian Development Bank.

Sen, J. 1969. The Jharkhand Movement', *Seminar on the Tribal Situation in India*. Shimla: Indian Institute of Advanced Study.

Sengupta, N. 1980. 'Caste and Tribals in Jharkandh', *Economic and Political Weekly,* 15(14): 664-71.

Sharma, K.L.1986. *Caste Class and Social Movements.* Jaipur: Rawat Publications.

Shashi S.S. *"Tribes of Andhra Pradesh"* Anmol Publication Pvt. Ltd; New Delhi, 1995.

Shyam Lal 2003 India 2003, *Compiled and edited by Research, References and Training Division,* Ministry of Information and Broadcasting, Government of India, 2003.

Singh Sundera 1998, *Tribal Development, Reflections and Remedies,* Social Welfare, Vol. 45, No. 8.

Singh, Anil Kumar, 1994, "Problems of Scheduled Castes and Scheduled Tribes", in Anil Kumar Singh(Ed) *Approaches to Tribal Development,* New Delhi, Sarup and Sons.

Singh, B. 1982(ed). Steps Towards Tribal Development. *The Third Step: Training of Trainers in Tribal Development Administration.* Delhi: Department Of Personal Administration, Govt. of India.

Singh, K.S. 1977. 'From Ethnicity to Regionalism: A Study of Tribal Politics and Movements in Chotanagpur from 1900 to 1975', in S.C.Malik (ed): *Dissent, Protest and Reform in Indian Civilisation* (317-43). Shimla: Indian Institute of Advanced Study.

Singh, K.S. 1982. *Tribal Movements in India*, Vol. 1, New Delhi: Manohar Publications.

Singh, K.S. 1983a. 'Introduction', in K.S.Singh (ed): *Tribal Movements in India,* Vol. 2. New Delhi: Manohar Publications.

Singh, K.S. 1983c. 'The Tribal Autonomy Movements in Chhotanagpur', in K.S.Singh (ed): *Tribal Movements in India*, Vol.2. New Delhi: Manohar Publications.

Singh, K.S. 2002. 'Tribal Autonomy Movements in Chhotanagpur', in Ghanshaym Shah (ed): *Social Movements and the State* (267-92). New Delhi: Sage Publications.

Singh, K.S., 1994, *People of India, National Services*, Vol.III. The Scheduled Tribes, Delhi, Oxford University Press.

Singh, R. 2001. *Social Movements, Old and New: A Post-Modernist Critique.* New Delhi: Sage Publications.

Singh, S. 2002. 'Tribal Solidarity Movements in India: A Review', in Ghanshyam Shah (ed): *Social Movements and the State* (251-66). New Delhi: Sage Publications.

Somasekhar K. & M. Bapuji, Credit System in Tribal Areas: Need for Re-orientation", *Kurukshetra*, Vol. 51, No. 4, February 2003, p. 22-26.

Subba Ramaraju, Sudhakar, *C. Developmental Programmes and Social Transfermattion.* Associated Publishers, New Delhi, 2006.

Sundarapandian M., *'Tribal Development in India'*, Anmol Publications, New Delhi, 2000.

Surnder sub: Rural Connectivity, Current Issues and Future Plants; *Kurukeshtra*, October, 2002.

Sushma Sahay 1998 Women and Empowerment Approaches and Strategies, Discovery Publishing House, 4831/24, Ansari Road Prahlad Street, Daryaganj, New Delhi-110002

Thakur, A. 2001. Tribal Development and Its Paradoxes. New Delhi: Authors Press.

Thariem, A.K., 2001, "Penspectives of Health For All in the 21st Century, *Bharatiya Samajik Chintan*", A Quarterly Journal of Social Sciences, Nos. 1-4, Vol. XXIV.

Thurston, E., *"Castes and Tribes of Southern India,"* Madras Government Press. 1909 rpt. 1975, Delhi Cosmo Publication Vol. 111, pp. 442-3.

Todaro, U.P., 1985, *"Economic Development in the Third World"*, Orient Longman, New Delhi.

Toppo, S.R. 2000 *Tribes in India,* Indian Publishers Distributors, Delhi.

Tripathy, S.N, 1998; Discovery Publishing House; Tribals in India: The Changing Scenario; Tara Dutt; Tribal Development in India; Orissa; Gyan Publishing House; 2001.

Umamohan, C. Naganna, A., "Yerukula Tribes and Social Transformation," Bharatiya Adimajathi Sevak Sangh (*Vanyagati*), New Delhi 2006.

Umamohan, C. A.Naganna, Educational Attainments and Empowerment of A Stigmatised Scheduled Tribe: An Inter-generational Study of Yerukula Tribe in Rayalaseema. *Paper Presented to the National Seminar,* Education and Social Empowerment, 5th and 6th July 2007, Dr. B. R. A. Open University, Hyderabad.

Umamohan, C. A. Naganna, Globalisation: Continuity and Change of Livelihood and Interdependence: A Study of Yerukula Tribe (*Paper Submitted at the National Seminar on Globalisation:* Indian Society, Continuities and Change Hyderabad, 7th April, 2006).

Umamohan, C. A.Naganna, Occupational Changes and Mobility: An Intra- Generational Study of Yerukulas in Rayalaseema Region of AP. *National Seminar on 3rd and 4th November*, 2006. Dravidian University, Kuppam.

Umamohan, C. A.Naganna, Perception and Assessment on Standard of Living, Quality of Life and Social Well-being: An Inter-generational Study of a Stigmatised Scheduled Tribe, the

Yerukulas in Rayalaseema Region of Andhra Pradesh *National Seminar on Tribal Development: A Myth or Pragmatic Reality?* 26th and 27th- February, 2007. Organised by Department of Anthropology Sri Venkateswara University, Tirupati.

Umamohan, C. A.Naganna, Reproductive Healthcare: An Inter-Generational Study of Yerukulas in Rayalaseema Region of AP. *National Seminar on 3rd and 4th November*, 2006, Dravidian University, Kuppam.

Umamohan, C. A.Naganna, Social Stigma and Yerukula Tribe: A Study of Social Exclusion and Inclusion. *Paper Presented to the International Seminar Social Exclusion and Inclusive Policies In South Asia* 17th to 19th March, 2008, Shivaji University, Kolhapur.

Upadhaya, A. 1980b. 'Class Struggle in Rural Maharastra, India: Toward a New Perspective', *The Journal of Peasant Studies,* vii (2):46-62.

Umamohan, C. A.Naganna, Social Stigma and Social Exclusion: A Study of Yerukula Tribe in Rayalaseema Region of Andhra Pradesh. *Paper Presented to the National Workshop, Social Exclusion and Inclusive Policy with Special Reference to Weaker Sections of India,* 28th to 29th March, 2008 Andhra University, Visakhapatnam.

Unpublished Monograph of TCRTI, Government of Andhra Pradesh.2000.And Rural Household Healthcare Needs and Availability, 1992.

Usha Mehata 1998. Indian Women and Their Participation in Politics, *Journal of the Council for Social Development,* Volume 8, No.3. September 1978.

Viduarthi, L.P. 1977. *The Tribal Culture of India.* Delhi: Concept Publishing Company.

Vidyarthi, L.P. 1981. *Tribal Development and Its Administration.* New Delhi: Concept Publishing House.

Vasudeva Rao, B.S., et.al. (2003): *'Evaluation Study'* Edited Volume, the Associated Publishers, Ambala Cantt.

Vasudeva Rao. D. (2000), *Pathology of Poverty (a Micro Level Study* in Andhra Pradesh), Council for Social Development, Hyderabad.

Vasudeva Rao. D. (2001), Democratic Common Interest Groups Foster Empowerment in Andhra Pradesh. *Social Welfare*, Vol. 47, No. 11, p. 27.

Venkttakumar, R and K.B.Sripal, "People's Participation: An Innovation to Incite Development", *Kurukshetra*.Vol.47, No.7, April 1999.

Venkat Rao, P, *Tribal Development: Policy and Practice;* 2001; Sarup and Sons.

Vasudeva Rao, B.S., 2003, *"Evaluation Studies"*, Associated Publishers, Ambala Cantt.

Workshop Proceedings (2002), *Andhra Pradesh Community Forest Management Project (Souvenir),* Forest Department, Government of Andhra Pradesh.

World Bank, 2006. *India: Inclusive Growth and Service Delivery Building on India's Success.* Macmillan India Ltd., Delhi.

Wiseman, John (Ed.). 1997. *Alternatives to Globalisation: An Asia-Pacific Perspective*. Melbourne: Community Aid Abroad.

INDEX

I

K

L

M

N

O

P

T

U